MOMENTS
THAT MATTER

MOMENTS
THAT MATTER

See, Shape, and Scale What Counts

Chris Dyer

ADVANCE PRAISE

"The most interesting thing Chris ever said to me became this book. I told him if he didn't write it, I would. He made the right call. He's given leaders permission to stop optimizing everything and start recognizing what actually matters."

Pete Sheahan, C-suite Advisor, Author, Serial Entrepreneur

"Leadership happens in moments. Chris Dyer has written a practical, research-backed guide to recognizing the moments that define your impact and showing up fully when they arrive."

Marshall Goldsmith, #1 *New York Times* Bestselling Author, Thinkers50 #1 Executive Coach

"Chris Dyer reminds us that impact isn't about doing more—it's about knowing when to show up, and how. This book offers a hard-earned, honest road map for choosing presence over performance and turning key moments into meaningful change."

Laura Gassner Otting, *Wall Street Journal* Bestselling Author of *Wonderhell*

"Less than 1 percent of our experiences make it into long-term memory. Chris Dyer's *Moments That Matter* teaches you how to create that 1 percent intentionally. Equal parts neuroscience and street-smart leadership wisdom, this book belongs on every leader's desk."

Josh Linkner, *New York Times* Bestselling Author, Five-Time Tech Entrepreneur, Venture Capital Investor

"*Moments That Matter* shows why leadership isn't defined by consistency alone but by how well we recognize and rise to moments of disproportionate impact. Grab a copy and read it so you can recognize these moments before your competitors do."

Brittany Hodak, Author of *Creating Superfans*

"Chris Dyer answers a question every leader should be asking: why do some interactions fade while others define careers, cultures, and relationships for decades? *Moments That Matter* gives you the framework to stop leaving your most important moments to chance. If you care about human-centered leadership and the impact you have on others, this book is a must read."

Ryan Estis, Bestselling Author of *Prepare for Impact*, Former Fortune 500 Chief Revenue Officer

"Leadership is about heart. And heart shows up in moments. Chris Dyer has written a practical guide to recognizing those moments and bringing your full self to them when they arrive."

Claude Silver, Chief Heart Officer, VaynerX

"In a world obsessed with speed and scale, this book makes a compelling case for something deeper: that leadership is shaped in moments, not systems. Practical, human, and deeply relevant for the future of work."

Seth Mattison, Bestselling Author of *The Future of Leadership*, named one of the Top 50 Keynote Speakers in the World

"Most leadership advice tells you to make every moment matter. This book does something far more useful: it teaches you to recognize the few moments that already do, and to show up for them with intention. It's a practical framework for creating outsized impact at work and at home, because in the end, people do not remember our routines. They remember our moments."

Dr. Shawn DuBravac, *New York Times* Bestselling Author

"Moments are where culture is built—and broken. *Moments That Matter* gives leaders a clear, practical way to show up for the moments that shape trust, commitment, and performance."

David Burkus, Author of *Best Team Ever*

"The leadership book that explains why some teams become unforgettable."

Robyn Benincasa, CNN Hero, World Champion Adventure Racer, Veteran Firefighter

"Moments That Matter reminds us that meaning isn't created by doing more. It's created by showing up when it counts. Habits are what steady us day to day, but moments define how we remember them. Chris Dyer provides a powerful guide to recognize those pivotal moments and have the resilience to meet them with presence and clarity."

Mandy Gill, Bestselling Author of *Reset with Resilience*, Founder of Hooked on Healthy Habits

"Monday is a moment. So is every decision, every transition, every truth we deliver to our teams. Chris Dyer has written the playbook for leaders who want to stop stumbling through these moments and start winning them with purpose, on purpose."

Paul Epstein, Former NFL and NBA Executive, Two-Time Bestselling Author, Founder and CEO of WIN MONDAY™

"Making the most of a moment when it shows up requires courage. Chris Dyer wrote the book that connects these two ideas in a way I hadn't read before. *Moments That Matter* will change how you think about leadership, relationships, and stewardship."

Ryan Berman, Founder of Courageous, Author

"AI will transform how we work. But it won't transform what makes work meaningful. Chris Dyer helps us to see the human side of high performance with clarity. He shows us the moments that build trust, create loyalty, and make people want to follow you. In a world racing toward automation, this book is more relevant than ever."

Dan Chuparkoff, Former Google and McKinsey Executive, CEO of Reinvention Labs

"Attention is our most valuable cognitive resource, yet many leaders are more distracted than ever. *Moments That Matter* helps you cut the noise and place your attention where it delivers the biggest return."

Dr. James Hewitt, Human Performance Scientist

"Moments define us. Chris Dyer teaches leaders how to stop stumbling through them and start owning them."

Chad E. Foster, Author of *Blind Ambition*, first blind executive to graduate from Harvard Business School's leadership program

"Relationships are your superpower. Chris Dyer shows you where to use it. The moments that matter don't raise their hands. Connection isn't constant. It's built in the moments we choose to truly show up."

Barb Betts, Keynote Speaker, Author, and Human Connection Expert

"Chris Dyer reveals something leaders often overlook: innovation and growth don't just happen in strategy sessions. They happen in moments. As someone who has researched this topic extensively, I can say that this book will change the way you approach your next challenge or goal because it teaches you to recognize the ones that matter and stop wasting the ones that don't."

Sheri Jacobs, Three-Time Bestselling Author, CEO of Avenue M Group

For my grandson, Niko.
Everything in these pages is what I want you to carry forward.
Everything you've given me is why it was worth writing down.

TABLE OF CONTENTS

Part Two: The Framework *Seven Moments That Control Everything: In Business, In Life, and In Relationships*

INTRODUCTION

"Make every moment matter." How many times have you heard that line? By now, you've probably run into it in the pages of books on business and leadership, across motivational social media posts, and on the insides of greeting cards.

Sure, it's well-intentioned advice. But it's also deeply unhelpful.

Trying to make *every* moment meaningful turns life into a performance, and work into a grind. It asks too much of us, and, paradoxically, it cheapens the moments that actually matter. When everything is urgent, nothing is important. When every interaction is treated like a defining one, we burn out, miss what's real, and lose sight of what truly moves people.

This book offers a different approach. It's a business book. And it isn't.

The principles in these pages work in boardrooms and living rooms. They apply to employees and children, to customers and neighbors, to the teams you lead and the friendships you're trying not to let fade. I've seen the same framework help a CEO redesign her onboarding experience and a father reconnect with his teenage son. I've watched it transform how a sales team approaches client relationships and how a woman shows up for a friend going through divorce.

You choose your arena. You decide which roles matter most.

Maybe it's being the best leader your employees will ever work for. Not a good leader, but rather the one they look back on decades later and say, "She changed my life." Maybe it's being the parent your kids remember as actually present. Maybe it's being the friend who shows up when everyone else just texts.

I won't ask you to be the best at everything. That way lies exhaustion. I will, however, ask you to recognize that, wherever you've decided to show up, moments are the currency of impact.

Not all moments are created equal. Some are worth a thousand days of consistency. Some can shatter years of accumulated trust. Neuroscience tells us that less than 1 percent of our experiences make it into long-term memory. But that tiny fraction shapes how we feel about entire chapters of our existence. Careers. Relationships. Identities.

This book will teach you to see those moments before they pass, shape them while they're happening, and scale their impact after they've occurred. You'll learn to recognize the seven universal moment types and use practical frameworks to show up when the stakes are highest. By the end, you'll be able to build cultures, at work and beyond, that are successful and functional but also healthy and meaningful for the people inside them. Cultures where people know when to push, when to pause, and when to show up fully because the moment demands it.

I've spent my career learning how to do that. Sometimes the hard way.

I spent two decades growing an idea into a company that functioned and then flourished. And then I sold it. Since then, I've consulted with hundreds of leaders who had sensed something was broken in their workplaces but couldn't quite name it. Again and again, the issue wasn't strategy or talent. It was missed moments. Rushed transitions. Avoided truths. Recognition that never landed. Culminations that went unmarked.

Everything I've learned from these experiences I've distilled into a simple but powerful idea: you don't need to make every moment matter. You need to know which moments really do. And recognizing, creating, and leveraging these moments will reshape the way you show up in every important relationship and will close the gap between who you are and who you want to be.

In part one, I dismantle the myths that have kept you from recognizing meaningful moments in real time and help you learn how to "take it hard" when easier but less impactful paths exist.

In part two, I introduce seven universal moment types and show you how to shape them so that they do the work they're capable of doing.

In part three, we turn those insights into practice, providing you with a playbook for auditing your organization's moments and building a culture in which people can recognize and create those moments on their own.

I share stories from my own life, including some I'm proud of and others I'm not. I've missed moments as a parent, burned people out by treating everything as urgent, and built a culture that couldn't survive my departure. These failures taught me more than my successes, and I'll be honest about both.

This book will not tell you to make every moment matter. Instead, it will help you distinguish between moments that deserve your full weight and those that don't. Because the goal isn't to make life heavier. It's to make it more meaningful.

When you learn to recognize the moments that matter most and show up for them on and with purpose, you don't just change outcomes. You change how people remember working with you, following your lead, and living alongside you.

That's the work ahead. And it starts by learning to see what's already right in front of you.

PART ONE: THE REVELATION

THE SECRET EVERYONE KNOWS BUT NOBODY USES

"Life is a succession of moments; to live each one is to succeed."

CORITA KENT

CHAPTER 1

THE DINNER THAT BROKE ME OPEN

It was a cold night in Oregon, and I was completely unprepared for it. I'm a California boy through and through, and my idea of cold-weather gear is throwing a light jacket in the car "just in case." So there I was, my latest keynote speech barely behind me, shivering my way through an unexpected reunion that would reshape everything I thought I knew about what really matters at work and in life.

The meeting over drinks was a time capsule decorated with a cocktail umbrella. In 2001, I started a human capital risk management and background-check software company called PeopleG2, and it was my whole world right up until I sold it in 2021. Now across the table from me were two people who'd been part of that journey. Tim had been a senior executive on my team, someone who'd helped build the company from the inside out. Sasha had been in customer service and was the kind of person who made clients feel like family.

Only minutes into drinks, it was like we'd never been apart. We laughed about the old days, the crazy client stories, the time we almost lost that huge account. Drinks turned into dinner, and dinner stretched into the evening.

When you sell a company, you tell yourself everyone's going to be fine, maybe even better off. These two certainly seemed to be. The new company had treated them well, they said. Both had gotten bonuses and promotions. Their careers were objectively better. By all accounts, we should have been celebrating.

After dinner, we decided to have one last drink. A toast, really, to this unexpected special occasion of being together again. That's when everything shifted.

"You know, we're still mad at you," Sasha said.

I laughed, assuming it was a joke. "What? What do you mean you're mad at me?"

"Yeah," Tim chimed in, nodding. "We're still really mad at you."

Their smiles were gone. This wasn't a joke.

"Do you mean," I replied slowly, "because I sold the company?"

Their answer was swift and synchronized.

"Yes."

I set down my drink, genuinely confused. "I don't understand," I replied. "You both got great bonuses because I sold the company. You've both gotten promotions. You're both making more money."

They looked at each other, then back at me.

"The work is different now," Tim began. Not just different. It was less. Less meaningful. Less energizing. Less authentic to who they are.

"It's not just about the new CEO," Sasha explained. "Of course, we miss you, but what we miss more is the way our teams used to work together. How we worked with clients. The direction we're heading in now feels very different."

So did the energy in the room when they solved problems. And the way they felt at the end of a tough week.

I felt like someone had reached into my chest and squeezed.

"But you're in a bigger organization now," I tried again. "You have more opportunities. You're making more money. Your career trajectories are..."

"Chris," Tim stopped me. "We would give back all the money to be working in the old company again."

His words hung there between us.

"That was the best work we've ever done in our careers," Sasha added. "That was the best of times."

I sat there, absolutely befuddled. These were smart people. Rational people. They were telling me they'd trade promotions, bigger salaries, better titles, more opportunities, all of it, to go back to what we'd had.

My initial reaction was one of amazement. Then, as I sobered up a bit, both literally and figuratively, something deeper hit me. They had just articulated what I'd been trying to say in my keynotes for years. I'd been up on stages talking about better culture, better engagement, making work not suck. But what I was really trying to get leaders to do, something I hadn't even fully understood myself, was to create an environment where people could do the best work of their careers.

"Tell me more," I appealed. "What made it the best?"

And that's when the real education began.

Tim and Sasha didn't talk about our ping-pong table. They didn't mention our flexible work policies or our health benefits or even the famous culture initiatives I'd written about in my books. Instead, they began telling me about *moments*. Specific, vivid moments that had happened years ago but felt like yesterday to them.

There was the moment when we almost lost our biggest client and instead of pointing fingers, the entire team stayed until 2 AM rebuilding the presentation from scratch. Not because anyone told them to but because it mattered.

There was the moment during the Texas power outages in February 2021 when the grid failed and millions lost heat in freezing temperatures. Within forty-eight hours, we'd bought generators for every affected employee, gave them paid time off without touching their PTO or vacation days, and encouraged them to help their neighbors and communities.

"I'll never forget how the company showed up when our families were literally freezing," Sasha revealed.

There was the moment when we landed that impossible account, the one everyone said we couldn't get. The spontaneous celebration that erupted wasn't about the commission checks. It was about proving we could do something nobody thought we could do.

There was the moment when I stood up in an all-hands meeting after we'd screwed up badly with a client. Instead of spinning it, I admitted, "We failed, and this is exactly how we're going to fix it and make sure it never happens again."

"In that moment," Sasha said, "I'd never respected anyone more."

"It wasn't the everyday stuff," Tim explained. "It was these moments when everything was on the line, when we could have folded or given up or played it safe, and we didn't. Those moments when we showed up as our best selves, not because we had to but because we wanted to."

Sasha jumped in. "Remember when that client's daughter was in the hospital and you flew out there just to sit with him? That wasn't in any employee handbook. But everyone saw it. Everyone knew that's who we were."

As they talked, a pattern emerged, one that would later become the foundation of everything I teach. Out of the thousands of days they'd worked at PeopleG2, they remembered maybe three to five specific moments with crystal clarity. They weren't the moments I'd tracked in performance reviews or the milestones on our strategic plans. They were human moments of disproportionate impact that had somehow encoded themselves into their permanent memory.

The neuroscience behind this is staggering. Our brains process approximately 11 million bits of information per second,[1] but less than 1 percent of our experiences make it into long-term memory.[2] That tiny fraction shapes how we feel about entire chapters of our lives, our relationships, our sense of who we are.[3] Those moments had made the cut.

What actually matters, it turns out, isn't what most organizations measure.

I drove back to my hotel that night with my mind spinning. These two successful professionals would trade money, titles, and career advancement to recapture something intangible: the feeling of doing their best work in an environment that brought out their best selves. How many other people felt this way? How many organizations were leaving this kind of impact on the table? How many families were missing these moments? How many friendships were fading because we weren't creating moments that mattered?

The implications extended beyond employee engagement. If certain moments have this kind of disproportionate impact, what about customers? What about the relationships that matter most to spouses, children, closest friends?

A few weeks later, I was in Denver with Pete Sheahan, who has coached such speakers as Brené Brown and Mel Robbins and also happens to be one of my favorite mentors. When I shared what had happened at that dinner, his eyes lit up.

"That's the most interesting thing you've ever said to me," he proclaimed.

For the next twenty-five minutes, we mapped it out. The connections flew fast. How Apple designs product unboxing to be a moment. How The Ritz-Carlton empowers every employee to create memorable moments for guests. How certain leaders become legendary not through consistent competence but in the ways they show up in crucial moments. How some brands build billion-dollar valuations on a handful of perfectly orchestrated customer moments. How the best parents aren't perfect every day but show up powerfully in the moments that shape their children's lives.

"You know what you're really talking about?" Pete observed. "You're talking about seeing, shaping, and scaling the moments that matter. Before, during, and after they happen."

That was it. The bridge from my personal revelation to a universal principle.

We've all been taught that success comes from consistency, from doing the right things day after day, building trust bit by bit. And yes, consistency matters. But what I learned that night is that not all moments hold the same power. Some moments add hours to your life. Some moments stop the clock entirely.

We're all in the business of moments, whether we know it or not. Every organization, every leader, every team, every family, every friendship is creating moments right now. The question is, are you creating them intentionally? Do you even know which moments matter? Can you recognize them when they're happening? Can you amplify their impact? Can you design them into your culture, your customer experience, your leadership practice, your family traditions, your personal relationships?

My former employees would trade their higher salaries because money wasn't the real currency of their experience. The real currency was moments. Moments of truth, moments of connection, moments of triumph, moments of vulnerability, moments of becoming who they were meant to be.

With practice, we can learn to see those moments before they happen, to shape them as they unfold, and to scale their impact after they've occurred. While we may still measure performance in quarters and years, we remember our lives in moments. And if you can master the architecture of moments, if you can become intentional about creating moments of disproportionate impact, you won't just improve performance, productivity, and retention. You'll transform lives. Including your own.

That cold night I reconnected with Tim and Sasha made for a memorable setting, but it was the warmth of recognition, that moment when they revealed what really mattered to them, that changed everything. They thought they were mad at me for selling the company. What they were really mad about was losing a place where moments like that could happen.

Your people feel the same way. Your customers, your family, your friends. They're not looking for steadily accruing signs of success. They're looking for moments that matter.

Will you give them those moments? Will you become a leader, an organization, a parent, a friend, a person who makes the most of the moments that matter?

That's the invitation. That's the promise. Performance, productivity, and retention will rise. But more importantly, much more importantly, people's lives will improve too.

Because in the end, life isn't measured in time. It's measured in moments. And not all moments are created equal.

"In any given moment, we have two options: to step forward into growth or step back into safety."
ABRAHAM MASLOW

CHAPTER 2

THE MARBLE JAR LIE (AND WHY IT'S KEEPING YOU SMALL)

Fifth grade. New school. No friends.

I had just left private school for public school, and everything was different. Private school had been small and predictable. Public school felt like being dropped into the middle of the ocean.

When the talent show sign-ups were posted, I saw an opportunity. Not to showcase some hidden talent. After all, I didn't have one. But to maybe, possibly, hopefully make some friends.

I signed up on a whim, so when the teacher in charge of the show asked me what I'd like to perform, I had no answer.

"I know a song that would be perfect for you," she offered, her pencil rhythmically drumming her clipboard.

I didn't need much convincing. By the end of the conversation, I was committed to Starship's "We Built This City."

Unsurprisingly, I didn't win the talent contest. I don't even remember if I was good. But that teacher saw something in me. Or maybe she just saw a lonely kid who needed a win. Either way, after the show, she told me and a few others about an opportunity in Hollywood. Turns out her son was a producer on a new show called *Puttin' on the Kids*, a children's version of the adult show *Puttin' on the Hits*.

I gave it a shot, and somehow, improbably, I made it through audition after audition. First round, second round, third, fourth, and then, like a musical miracle, I made it to the actual TV taping. I was the only kid from my school to land that coveted spot.

You'd think my memorable moment would have happened during filming, right? The lights glimmering above me. The thrill and sweat of my performance. Finishing in third place behind the two co-champions of the series who had each managed to receive perfect scores.

But that wasn't the moment.

The moment was in the green room before the show. My Uncle Lee was there.

He wasn't supposed to be. He had lung cancer, and everyone had dutifully prepared me for his absence. But there he was, sitting in that cramped, fluorescent-lit room that smelled like hairspray mixed with anticipation.

We didn't talk about anything profound. He asked about my arm, the one I'd broken the year before falling off Rick, the more spirited of his two horses. Rick and Jerry were beautiful American Saddlebreds, and he loved them more than he did most people. My arm had healed nicely, and I told him so. Then he asked me about school. You know, normal stuff. Uncle stuff.

In fifth grade, I didn't understand that showing up when you have lung cancer is an act of love that transcends logic, but I did know how glad I was to have him there in that green room with me before the big show. Sometimes the moment you think matters is just the container for the moment that actually matters. That was the last time I saw Uncle Lee.

He died a few months later. But first, he watched me lip-sync on television. The cameras caught him in the audience, and there's this split second when you can see him, where he's preserved forever in that moment, one smiling uncle in a sea of faces.

That's the moment inside the moment. The performance was what we thought mattered. But the real moment, the one that locked itself into my permanent memory, was a dying man choosing to show up for his nephew.

The Lie We've All Been Told

It took me a long time to fully grasp what Uncle Lee had meant to teach me in that moment. Before I could get there, I had to let go of a powerful metaphor that shaped the way I thought about consistency and its role in my relationships. Maybe it's one you've been holding onto as well.

It comes from Brené Brown.

I've seen Brené speak at least twelve times. I love how she charts her own evolution, explaining exactly how she combined great research and real-world experience as she climbed to CEO. As she admits in *Daring Greatly*, research rarely looks the same when it's applied practically.[4]

In it, she introduced the world to the idea of the marble jar, which really resonated with me. Trust is built slowly, one small act at a time, like dropping marbles into a jar. Each time someone shows up consistently, another marble goes in. Each broken promise takes one out. Over time, the jar fills up, and you have trust. Daily consistency creates psychological safety.

Other great minds have built on this basic idea. In *The Power of Moments*, for example, authors Chip and Dan Heath identify four elements beyond consistency that contribute to memorable peaks: elevation, insight, pride, and connection.[5] Relationship researcher John Gottman added yet another layer: you need five positive interactions in order to overcome one negative. Five to one. That's the ratio for a healthy relationship.[6]

They're all right. But they're all missing something massive.

Uncle Lee didn't show up consistently. He showed up when it mattered. He showed up dying. And that single moment overwrote every marble that could have gone into any jar.

Yes, daily consistency matters, but it won't save you when the big moment arrives. You need both. You need the foundation of trust *and* the ability to recognize when you're inside a moment that will define everything.

Figure 2.1. The boulder and the marble jar.

For my first eight years running PeopleG2, I was terrible at this. I wasn't looking for moments. I was just reacting to whatever was happening. In so doing, I completely missed opportunities to show others I cared, that I was trustworthy, that our company was worth believing in.

There was a time, for instance, when I had the opportunity to hire an experienced salesperson in our industry. But I didn't. Because I didn't know him that well and because his salary demands were significantly more than I was prepared to handle. In that moment, though, I should have taken the shot and bet on the guy with experience. Instead, I focused on my immediate reality: he was too expensive, and I was just making things work.

As things tend to go, he went to our competitor. For years, he beat us on contracts. Deal after deal, we'd compete and lose. If he had done half as well with us as he did with them, we would have tripled our business. My fear of paying a larger salary probably cost us millions in revenue over the next decade.

That missed moment wasn't a failure of consistency. It was a failure of recognition. I couldn't see what was actually at stake.

The Boeing Problem

The more I thought about it, the more the marble jar metaphor started to dissolve. If trust is just about accumulating positive interactions, I wondered, how can one negative exchange or event destroy an entire relationship? Or brand image, for that matter?

Consider, for example, Boeing, a company that operated so reliably for so long that consumer trust was practically a given. That is until two crashes destroyed decades of good faith.

The 737 MAX had completed thousands of successful flights. Millions of passengers had arrived safely. Yet two crashes collectively ending 346 lives obliterated all of it.[7] Not just trust but Boeing's market value, reputation, entire narrative. The

House Transportation Committee's report revealed how Boeing's response made matters worse. The company downplayed problems, resisted grounding the fleet, and prioritized financial concerns over transparency. To consumers, the moment after the moment mattered just as much as the moment itself.[8]

Every airline CEO I've talked to since brings up the same thing. For decades, airlines chose Boeing because they trusted the company. And in a few poorly managed moments, that trust was gone. Not diminished. Gone. The daily deposits didn't matter when the moment arrived.

Uncle Lee understood this instinctively. He could have sent a card. He could have called. Those would have been marbles in the jar. Instead, he showed up when doing so cost him everything. Forty years later, I can't recall a single gift or card I received in the fifth grade, but I remember Uncle Lee.

The marble jar isn't wrong. It's just incomplete.

The Power of Awareness

Awareness changes everything. The fact that you're aware of the power of moments sets you up to take advantage when the right moment happens. Your ability to recognize these inflection points means you can show up big when they arrive. You become the calm in the center of the storm, the steady presence in the midst of chaos.

This awareness is what separates my Uncle Lee's choice from a mere visit. Somewhere, consciously or not, he recognized that this wasn't just another talent show. This was a moment that mattered. And he showed up despite the cost.

This awareness is what I finally developed after years of missing opportunities, burning people out, and rushing through parenthood. Once you see moments for what they are, you can't unsee them.

The Counterintuitive Truth

This brings me to a point that might upset some of you, especially if you're a fan of feel-good leadership books.

Not all moments are positive. And forcing them to be will keep you from greatness.

Michael Jordan understood this. During the 1995 Bulls training camp, Phil Jackson had Steve Kerr and Jordan guard each other in a scrimmage. They were going at it hard: trash-talking, fouling, competing like it mattered. Jackson started calling ticky-tack fouls to calm things down, trying to protect Kerr from Jordan's intensity.

Jordan got frustrated. In his words, as recorded in the documentary *The Last Dance*, "For you to be protecting this guy, that's not gonna help us when we play New York. It's not gonna help us when we play these teams that are very physical."[9]

The next foul, Jordan snapped. Kerr had thrown a punch to Jordan's chest, and Jordan responded by punching him in the eye. Phil threw Jordan out of practice immediately.

Then it got interesting. Jordan, upon reflection, called himself an idiot. He stood in the shower thinking, "I just beat up the littlest guy on the court," and he felt terrible. He called Kerr to apologize.[10]

But Kerr? He later said that the punch from Jordan was one of the best things that ever happened to him. "I needed to stand up and go back at him," he revealed. "I think I earned some respect." According to Kerr, their relationship "dramatically improved" after that punch. Their trust went to another level.[11]

Two years later, in Game 6 of the 1997 NBA Finals, with the championship on the line, Jordan did something almost unthinkable. During the timeout, knowing that the Jazz would double-team him, Jordan told Kerr to be ready. And when they did, Jordan, the man who always wanted the last shot, passed to Kerr.

Kerr nailed it. The Bulls won the championship.

The punch wasn't a positive moment. It was violent, shocking, and completely inappropriate by any HR standard. But it was a moment of truth that created something trust-building never could: respect forged in fire. Jordan and Kerr went 191–40 in games they played together, winning 82.7 percent of them. That doesn't happen without the kind of trust that transcends the typical exercises.

The Beautiful Prison of Small Thinking

I've worked with hundreds of companies, and I see the same pattern across industries. We've become so obsessed with preventing negative moments that we've forgotten how to create transformative ones.

We've built entire systems around incremental trust-building. Employee handbooks that run hundreds of pages. Policies for everything. Recognition programs that distribute praise like participation trophies. We measure engagement scores and satisfaction ratings and net promoter scores, all trying to add positive interactions to our jars, all trying to prevent their loss.

But what if that's exactly the trap?

In *Change or Die*, Alan Deutschman reveals something stunning about human nature. In a poignant case study, he follows patients who've undergone coronary bypass surgery. People who have literally been cracked open and given a second chance at life. Their doctors tell them explicitly: change your diet and exercise habits or you will die. Not might die. Will die.

You'd think the threat of death would be the ultimate motivator. I'd certainly expect a staring contest with mortality to spur lasting change. But that's not what happens. Instead, 90 percent of patients fail to change the behaviors that have led to their heart problems in the first place.[12]

Ninety percent.

These aren't people lacking information. They know exactly what to eat, how to exercise, what medications to take. They have support groups, nutritionists, cardiac rehabilitation programs. Everything except the ability to change when it matters most.

If the literal threat of death doesn't create lasting behavioral change, what chance does your quarterly business transformation have? What hope does your "critical" initiative carry when people won't even change in order to save their own lives?

This is why manufactured urgency fails. When everything is urgent, nothing is.

The Corporate Manifestation

I learned this lesson personally before I watched it destroy companies. But I still see it everywhere: companies burying their employees in pseudo-urgent tasks and goals as if they too are marbles that add up to productivity.

I recently consulted with a tech company that had been in "crisis mode" for three straight years. Every quarter had a new "bet the company" initiative. Every product launch was "existential."

The CEO genuinely believed that he was creating urgency. What he'd actually created was alarm fatigue. One engineering manager put it perfectly: "When everything is an emergency, nothing is. We're just standing in the middle of a burning building, wondering if this is Tuesday or Wednesday."

The urgency narrative took different names but echoed the same empty siren. It was "our moonshot moment" in January, "our D-Day invasion" in March, and "our Everest summit" in May. By June, his employees just called it Tuesday.

The irony? While treating everything as urgent, the company had missed three actual inflection points: a client request that would have opened a new market, a fundamental architecture problem flagged by an engineer, and a competitor pivot that would eventually eat half their market share.

It's exactly as researchers Erin M. Reid and Lakshmi Ramarajan documented in *Harvard Business Review*. Urgency culture creates people who are always in motion but are rarely making progress on what actually matters.[13]

The Warning

Let me be clear: do not make everything a burning platform. It's far more valuable to recognize which moments actually matter and meet them with the weight they deserve.

The research on "urgency fatigue" is clear. When companies operate in constant crisis mode, employees exhibit the same symptoms as combat veterans do: hypervigilance, exhaustion, and emotional numbing. Your brain cannot sustain that level of activation. It starts ignoring the alarms. Everything becomes background noise.[14]

That's what happens when you cry wolf with urgency. People stop running. They stop caring. They just shrug and think, *must be Tuesday*.

When leaders label everything as urgent, they're not prioritizing. They're abdicating responsibility and disseminating pressure without making the hard choices.[15]

This is what I call moment inflation. When every meeting is "crucial," every deadline is "critical," every project is "make or break," you haven't created urgency. You've destroyed discernment.

The companies that burned out trying to make everything matter? They missed the three or four moments that actually did matter. They were so busy adding positive interactions and declaring platforms on fire that they didn't notice the real moments of transformation standing right in front of them.

Making the Choice

As Uncle Lee taught me, the trust-building framework is real, but it's not enough. While daily consistency matters, it won't save you when the moment arrives. You need both. You need the foundation of trust *and* the courage to recognize and rise to the moments that will define everything.

It's true in neuroscience, and it's true in business and in life. Only a fraction of your experiences will make it to permanent storage in your memory. The ones that do aren't random. They follow patterns. They have identifiable characteristics. They can be created, shaped, and scaled.[16]

But first, you have to stop believing that it's all about incremental trust-building.

When in doubt, remember Boeing. Remember Tim and Sasha from that cold, late-night conversation that changed everything for me. All those positive marbles you've accumulated, whether from years of reliable service or promotions and bigger paychecks, won't matter a lick when weighed against defining moments.

This isn't feel-good philosophy. This is hard science meeting a harder truth. Research on memory consolidation shows that emotional intensity, not frequency, determines what gets locked into long-term memory. Your brain tags certain experiences as "worth remembering," and those become the stories we tell ourselves about our lives, our work, our relationships.[17]

You already know this. Think about your own career. You don't remember every day of your first job. You remember the day you got it. The day you quit. The day your boss said something that changed how you saw yourself. The day you succeeded when everyone thought you'd fail.

Three to five moments. Out of thousands of days.

What if you could identify those moments before they happened? What if you could create them intentionally? What if you could help others recognize when they're standing in one?

These are questions worth exploring. But they require us to ditch the lie that everything matters equally. Instead, we must embrace the transformative truth that a few moments matter disproportionately. Not because we lit a false fire to make them seem more urgent than they really are but because we all have experienced and will experience inflection points in our wondrous, winding lives.

The Invitation to Grow

Uncle Lee never knew he was creating one of the defining moments of my childhood. He was just showing up for his nephew. But his choice to be there when it could cost him everything taught me something I wouldn't understand for decades: the moment you think you're creating is rarely the moment that actually gets created.

You think you're competing in a talent show, but the moment is actually about the person who shows up for it.

You think you're building trust with daily consistency, but the moment is actually about what happens when that consistency gets tested.

You think you're managing performance with metrics, but the moment is actually about how you respond when the metrics fail.

It isn't that Brené Brown and the Heaths and John Gottman are wrong. They're right. The sacred cow I'm challenging is that their frameworks are sufficient. They're not.

After years of missing moments myself, I realized I'd been playing it safe. You probably have been too. We've been so afraid of the negative that we've avoided the transformative. We've been so focused on accumulating positive interactions that we've missed the moments that make those interactions irrelevant.

I've been there. I've been the guy missing moments, creating false urgency, rushing through life. If I can learn to see the moments that matter, to create them, to show up for them, so can you.

When psychologist Abraham Maslow said we can "step forward into growth or step back into safety," he was talking about moments. Specific moments when the choice to step forward changes everything.[18]

Your Uncle Lee moments are coming. The question is will you recognize them? Will you create them? Will you show up for them even when it costs you everything?

Because that's what the people in your life will remember. Not the consistency. Not the policies. Not the everyday reliability, as important as that is.

They'll remember the moments you chose to make matter.

"The cave you fear to enter
holds the treasure you
seek."

JOSEPH CAMPBELL

CHAPTER 3

THE TAKE-IT-HARD REVOLUTION

The plane was supposed to be zooming over Columbus, maybe Toronto, on a path that would arc over the Atlantic toward Moscow. Instead, we were circling above San Francisco for the second time, liquid streaming from the wings like a waterfall.

It was May 2007, and my wife Jody and I were strapped into the worn seats of an Aeroflot flight that made Spirit Airlines look like a luxury carrier. This was our fifth trip to Russia in eleven months, and we knew the drill by now: the smell of old upholstery mixed with industrial cleaning solution, the overhead bins that didn't quite close, the flight attendants who looked like they'd rather be anywhere else. But this trip was different. We were going to complete our family, to bring home Luba, the little girl whose hair my wife had braided at the orphanage just months earlier.

I can still see my son's face in the car that day, turning to us with the matter-of-fact certainty that only a seven-year-old can muster: "So are we going to adopt Luba or what?"

Going from zero to three kids in eleven months was already what I'd started calling "taking it hard," choosing the difficult path when an easier one existed. But what happened on that plane would teach me something deeper about what it means to choose difficulty when everything inside you screams for comfort.

The liquid cascading down from the wings was the first thing that got our attention. Then we noticed that the flight attendants had vanished. I'm convinced they had parachutes and a trap door hidden somewhere because we never saw them again for the rest of the flight. An engineer sitting three rows ahead turned around, his face pale, and said what we were all thinking but afraid to voice: "I think they might be dumping fuel."

In that pre-smartphone era, we pulled out our PalmPilots and BlackBerries and craned them desperately toward the windows, trying to get a signal. The small screens stayed dark. We were alone up there with our fear, 35,000 feet above the known world, with no way to tell anyone what was happening.

The cabin transformed into something I'd never experienced before. Fear has a smell: sharp, metallic, part sweat and part that peculiar staleness of recycled airplane air. People started spiraling, but in the strangest way. We'd lost three engines. We were dumping fuel down onto the nondescript blue below us that was the Pacific Ocean. We might die. But nobody wanted to talk about that.

Instead, they fixated on the fuel dumping itself.

"They're killing all the fish!" a woman two rows back protested.

"There's no predicting the extent of the environmental damage," said a man near the front, whose frustration had propelled him to his feet. "It's unconscionable."

People who'd probably never given a second thought to marine ecology were suddenly passionate environmentalists, furious about the impact on ocean life.

It was safer to be angry about fish, I realized, than to face the possibility we might not make it to Moscow. Their terror had to go somewhere, and somehow the entire plane had unconsciously agreed that environmental outrage was more manageable than mortal fear was. The whole cabin was becoming a pressure cooker of misdirected panic, 300 people arguing about anything except the reality that we had one working engine and twelve hours of flight ahead of us.

I unbuckled my seat belt and started to stand. Someone had to do something.

My wife, seeing this, grabbed my forearm with both hands, her fingernails piercing the knit of my sweater. "You're not in charge," she mouthed.

"But I can help," I insisted.

She released my arm, but unhappily. I stood and faced my fellow passengers.

"Hey, everyone," I said.

What answered me was a sudden and unexpected silence. Three hundred pairs of eyes turned toward me. The arguing stopped. The nervous chatter ceased. The whole plane fell into the hush, waiting.

Sometimes just trying to lead, to help, is enough. People will respond. I'd done it enough in the past to know that the passengers would give me a chance. Or at least hear me out. Either way, I had to try. If I could bring them back to our immediate reality, I could remind them of what was most important.

"We have to dump the fuel," I explained, my voice steadier than I felt.

The arguments erupted immediately. The environment. The fish. The waste. I realized I had to be more direct, get really specific with them about what actually mattered in that terrifying moment suspended between California and catastrophe.

"If we don't dump the fuel, we're going to die."

The silence that followed was different than before. This wasn't the quiet of attention; it was the silence of understanding.

Then something extraordinary happened. The little *babushka* sitting next to me, this traditional Russian grandmother with her floral headscarf, thick accent, and, I'd assumed, no English, stood up slowly. She couldn't have been more than five feet tall, but in that moment, she filled the entire plane. She looked at everyone, waited for complete attention, and in the pin-drop silence uttered, "Forget the fish."

Except she didn't say *forget*. She used a word that also starts with "f" and would have made my mother wash my mouth out with soap.

She created understanding with just three words. Three words and 300 terrified people instantly understood that there was something more important than the fish, more important than arguing, more important than anything except landing that plane safely.

We'd lost three of our four engines. We had enough fuel for the twelve-and-a-half-hour flight to Moscow, but that was now out of the question. When we finally touched down at LAX, twenty-five fire trucks and ambulances were arranged along the runway like a tragic welcoming committee, ready to scrape us off the tarmac. In the end, though, we landed safely.

Inside the airport, the rest of my fellow passengers tried to follow me through customs and to the ticket counter as if I knew what I was doing, as if standing up in that moment had somehow made me their leader.

I could have stayed in my seat. I could have let everyone spiral deeper into panic while I held my wife's hand and minded my own business. That would have been taking it easy. Instead, I stood up. No training in crisis management. No authority from the airline. Just a choice to take it hard when the moment demanded it.

That choice to stand up when sitting down would have been safer connects to everything I've learned since about moments that matter. Sometimes taking it hard means being willing to lead when you have no authority. Sometimes it means advocating when everyone tells you to accept. Sometimes it means investing when everyone else retreats. The thread that connects them all is recognizing when a moment matters more than your comfort.

When Taking It Hard Saves Lives

Four years later, on a Saturday morning that started like hundreds of others, I was standing on the sideline of a soccer field watching one of the kids play soccer, which was a bit more like organized chaos than an intentional act. Russia's January cold seemed like a lifetime ago. The Southern California sun was already warm at 9 AM when my wife mentioned her neck hurt.

"Slept wrong," she explained, rotating her head slowly, trying to work out the stiffness.

After the game, we distributed juice boxes and orange slices, corralled three sweaty kids into the car, and made it home in time for lunch. Only then did my wife decide to try seeing a chiropractor. She'd never been to one before, but several friends swore by theirs. It seemed like such a small decision at the time.

That afternoon, she went to her appointment and then on to Nordstrom afterward for some quick shopping. When she called me from the parking lot, her voice was shaking.

"Something's wrong," she said. "The whole world is spinning."

That was likely the first stroke, but we didn't know it then.

She made it home somehow. Later, while getting ready for dinner with friends, she was putting on earrings, small silver hoops she loved, when it happened again. The room tilted violently. She grabbed the dresser to steady herself, suddenly dizzy and nauseous. She sat down on the edge of our bed, and I watched the confusion in her eyes turn to fear.

"Something's really wrong," she said.

That was stroke number two.

We were still hours away from understanding what was happening to her.

The emergency room at our local hospital was quiet for a Saturday night. The doctors seemed puzzled but not particularly concerned. Inner ear infection and vertigo, they concluded after running some basic tests. Go home and rest and follow up with your doctor.

But I saw the way the left side of her face wasn't moving quite right, the way her words came out just slightly slurred, like she'd had one glass of wine too many, except she hadn't had anything to drink.

"Could this be a stroke?" I asked the attending physician.

He was a young guy, and he looked like he'd been on shift too long. When he processed my question, he actually laughed. Not cruelly, but with the confidence of someone who knew better.

"She's thirty-three years old," he said finally. "She's a former college athlete. Look at her. Does she look like a stroke patient to you?"

We went home.

At 3 AM, I woke to a repeated thud on the floor. My wife was trying to reach the bathroom, but with every step, she'd fall to one side, as if gravity had shifted and was pulling her horizontally instead of down. When she tried to speak, tried to tell me what was happening, her words came out jumbled, like someone had taken the sentence apart and reassembled it in the wrong order.

We went straight back to the emergency room. This time, they admitted her.

While my wife slept in her hospital bed, I stayed by her side, beating away at the keys of an ancient Dell computer, hoping it might provide a fuller picture of what was happening. Everything I read pointed to one possibility: the chiropractic adjustment had caused a stroke. It was all there beneath my blinking cursor. The twisting, the neck manipulation, the immediate symptoms afterward. What else could it be?

When I found the doctor on call and shared my theory, she didn't laugh. She agreed it was possible, even probable. But this was a small local hospital. Their MRI machine didn't run on weekends. We'd have to wait until Monday for definitive answers.

"What can we do now?" I asked.

"Well, if she had a stroke, we'd want to put her on blood thinners to prevent another one," the doctor advised, her voice calm and measured.

"Then why can't we start that now?"

They couldn't give my wife medicine until they knew what was wrong with her, she explained. As did the next doctor. And the next. For the next two hours, I argued with a parade of physicians who empathized but agreed. There was nothing to do until my wife was tested, and the test wasn't available.

Besides, there were other theories. My wife had a history of ulcers, so they wanted to do an endoscopy to see if there might be a link. Inner ear problems were another possible cause. Blood tests were ordered to rule out infection. Yes, stroke presented a larger risk, but the doctors only saw a young, healthy woman who couldn't possibly be having a stroke.

For two hours, I pushed. I advocated. I refused to accept the easy answer and "just wait until Monday." I spent every minute of those two hours as *that guy*, the difficult family member who just wouldn't accept what he was told.

Finally, around 6 AM, one doctor, an older woman who'd been listening from the doorway, stepped forward.

"I'll authorize the blood thinners," she said simply.

That moment, that decision to take it hard when taking it easy would have been so much simpler, probably saved my wife's life.

When Monday morning came, our family doctor, a man we'd trusted for years, came in shaking his head. "There's no way this is a stroke," he proclaimed with the confidence of thirty years of practice. "I'll eat my shoe if she's had a stroke. She's too young, too healthy, too everything."

The MRI showed she'd had three strokes. Three. A vertebral artery dissection from the neck adjustment had torn the delicate lining of the artery feeding her brain.

I had chosen not to just accept what I was being told by people who supposedly knew better but didn't have all the facts and instead push harder for what my instincts said was right. Taking it hard meant trusting those instincts even when experts disagreed.

The Longer Road

The months that followed redefined what "difficult" meant for our family. There were seemingly endless rounds of both physical and occupational therapy. My wife, who'd been a straight-A student her entire life, who'd played college basketball, who could solve complex problems in her sleep, now had to relearn so many things.

Every single day, she faced the same choice I'd faced on that plane and in the hospital: take it easy, accept the limitations, let others handle it. Or take it hard: fight for every word, every movement, every piece of herself she wanted back.

And get it back she did!

Then came the headaches. Not ordinary headaches but violent, debilitating, crushing pain that only eased when she lay completely flat. Back to the hospital, back to doctors who seemed perpetually confused by her case. This time, they insisted on a lumbar puncture to test for meningitis.

In that moment, I failed. I didn't ask the right questions: what's the probability she has meningitis? Less than 5 percent. What's the chance of complications from a lumbar puncture while she's on blood thinners? It's much higher: 15 to 20 percent.

She didn't have meningitis. But the lumbar puncture had caused a cerebrospinal fluid leak that would require surgery to repair. That leak was fixed, but we discovered that there had been another leak, likely caused by the same damage that gave her the strokes. Surgeries two, three, and four were not successful. She'd spent months on recovery and rehabilitation and was finally getting back to work, only to start all over again.

Through all of this, she kept working. With headaches that no painkiller could touch, that only lying flat could ease, she still went to her job. Partly because work gave her purpose when her body was failing her. But mostly because if she stopped, we'd lose the insurance that gave us access to Dr. Wouter Schievink at Cedars-Sinai, one of only a handful of specialists in the world who understood cerebrospinal fluid leaks.

The fifth surgery was something out of science fiction. Finally, a new, state-of-the-art machine could more accurately find where her leak was located using live-action, real-time CT imaging known as fluoroscopy. The leak was in a location that couldn't be accessed through her spine, so they'd have to go through her chest to repair it.

During the surgery, a cardiothoracic surgeon removed her heart, literally removed it, and kept her stable while Dr. Schievink found and repaired the leak. Then the cardiac team put her heart back in and sewed her up. She was one of the first people to have this procedure.

During that fifth surgery, while she was unconscious on the operating table, a visiting surgeon from Japan examined her neck and delivered devastating news: all the surgical trauma might cause her neck to become unstable as she ages. Without reinforcement, it could snap when she was in only her sixties or seventies.

I had to decide, right there in the ICU, whether to authorize another surgery, a procedure to stabilize her neck. If you are keeping score, this would be surgery number six. My wife was asleep on the table. I had no way to consult with her, to ask her what she wanted.

I stood in that consultation room, staring into the scans that documented her spinal damage. *This is what taking it hard really means*, I thought. It wasn't just fighting for what you want. Sometimes it's making impossible choices for someone you love when they can't make them for themselves.

"Do it," I told the doctors. They performed that surgery the next morning.

When my wife woke up three days later, I had a lot to fill her in on. For starters, her primary surgery had been successful. But there was more. She'd also had a second surgery she didn't even know she needed.

Advocating for my wife in the hospital taught me so much about what it means to enter a situation prepared to take it hard. The doctors who ran out of the room whenever I had a question? The ones who wouldn't have real conversations or who were afraid to admit uncertainty? Those were the ones to avoid. The doctors who would sit down with me, who would admit, "I don't know, but let's figure it out," who would entertain the hundreds of hours of research I'd done? Those were the doctors who ultimately saved her.

I spent those hundreds of hours reading medical journals, learning terminology I never wanted to know, understanding procedures I wished I'd never heard of. Not because I enjoyed it. Not because it was easy. But because when the moment came to advocate for my wife, I needed to be the most prepared nonmedical person in the room. I needed to ask the hard questions, push back against consensus, even when doctors rolled their eyes, even when nurses whispered about "that difficult husband."

Taking it hard in those moments meant being willing to be difficult when being easy might cost everything. It meant doing all the prep work in anticipation of the moments that would follow, the ones that mattered the most. It meant being ready to embrace discomfort in order to reach the relief on the other side.

The Business of Taking It Hard

The same principle that made me stand up on a plane and fight with doctors showed up in my business life, though the stakes were certainly different. Not life and death but livelihood and legacy.

Before he cofounded Netflix, Reed Hastings was CEO of Pure Software, a company he'd built into a successful debugging software firm. But Hastings recognized something most CEOs won't admit: he wasn't the right person to take the company to the next level.

So he fired himself. He didn't lean into a long and gentle transition. He fired himself as CEO and brought in someone else, and eventually the company merged with Rational Software. Most people would have held on. Hastings chose to take it hard.

He spent the next two years thinking about what went wrong. Those lessons became the foundation of Netflix.[19]

Taking it hard sometimes means making the right choice even when it requires sacrifice. Even when it means giving up the company you've built. Even when everyone else thinks you're crazy.

I faced my own version of this choice in 2009. The Great Recession had everyone in business running scared. My competitors in the background-check industry weren't just cautious; they were in full retreat. They cut their marketing budgets by 40 percent. They laid off sales staff. They hoarded cash and pulled back from trade shows, conferences, anything that cost money. They battened down the hatches and waited for the storm to pass.

I saw something different. I saw empty space where my competitors used to be.

My company increased its marketing spend by 30 percent. We transformed every employee into a sales contributor.

Customer service listened for hiring needs. Even IT got involved by researching prospects.

We became one of the first companies in our industry to use video email marketing. In 2009, embedding video in an email was revolutionary. We sent thousands, showing up when everyone else disappeared.

My team thought I was reckless. My competitors thought I was desperate. My CFO kept showing me the cash burn rate, the marketing costs, the risk we were taking.

But I knew something they didn't seem to grasp: the economy wasn't going to stop. Even in the worst recession since the 1930s, companies still hired people. Less than before? Yes. More carefully? Absolutely. But they still hired. And when they did, which would they remember? The company that vanished when things got tough or the one that stayed visible, stayed helpful, stayed present?

It didn't work immediately. For six months, we bled money while our competitors sat on their cash reserves, smug in their caution. But as companies started to breathe again, as hiring slowly resumed, we were top of mind. We'd been there during the darkness. We'd kept talking when everyone else had gone silent. We'd taken it hard when taking it easy seemed like the only sensible choice.

By 2011, we'd doubled our market share. Several competitors never recovered.[20]

Taking it hard in business meant the same thing it meant on that plane and in those hospital rooms: being willing to act when others wouldn't, to push when others pulled back, to stand up when sitting down would have been so much safer.

The Third Space and High Sensory Tuning

Often, being able to make the right choices when you're inside a big moment requires you to do some advance preparation. I could not have successfully advocated for my wife in the hospital, for example, if I hadn't spent hours and hours educating

Figure 3.1. The Third Space between where you were and where you're going.

myself on the relevant medicine. The moment *before* the moment can be every bit as important as the moment itself.

I call this period the "Third Space."[21] It's the preparation zone that exists before the crucial moment arrives, the place where you decide not just what you'll do but who you'll be when everything is on the line.

The Third Space is where you decide: am I showing up as the advocate or the bystander? It's where you prepare not just your words but also your entire presence.

Think about the best negotiators you know. They spend exponentially more time preparing than actually negotiating. They research everything about the other party, not just their business needs but also their personal style, their pressure points, their definition of success. They write out every possible objection and craft responses. They rehearse until the words feel natural. They get into character like actors preparing for the role of their lives, because in that moment, that's exactly what they're doing: performing the role of their lives.

My big role came when my wife's life was on the line. While doctors rushed from patient to patient, each case just a pause in their daily parade of crises, I could make them stop and think differently because I'd done the work in the Third Space. I'd done my research and prepared my questions, but I also prepared my presence, my conviction, my refusal to be dismissed.

But the Third Space isn't just about preparation. It's also about what I call High Sensory Tuning: the ability to regulate your internal state so you can actually sense what's happening in the moment, not just what you expect or fear is happening.

I have a new mantra of late: "The universe is conspiring in my favor." When people first hear this, they usually laugh, yet many go on to adopt it for themselves. It sounds like wishful thinking until you understand what it really means. When you believe that good outcomes are possible, that solutions exist even if you can't see them yet, that the moment can unfold in ways that serve everyone, you show up differently. You ask different questions. You notice different opportunities. You create space for something extraordinary to happen instead of forcing your predetermined outcome.

High Sensory Tuning means believing you can create the right conditions for a great outcome without manipulating or controlling exactly what that outcome will be. It's the difference between walking into a hospital room determined to force doctors to prescribe blood thinners and walking in ready to advocate for the best possible care, whatever that might be. The first approach creates resistance. The second creates possibility.

This combination of preparation and presence, of doing the work beforehand and then being fully attuned in the moment, is what allows you to take it hard when it matters most.

The Moment Recognition Pattern

After years of missing moments and then finally learning to see them, I've discovered they follow a predictable pattern. They almost always announce themselves through three signals:

1. **Physical Signal.** Your body knows first. You might have an elevated heart rate. Or sweaty palms. Or just a feeling in your chest that says, "This matters." On the plane, my body was screaming at me to act before my mind caught up. In the hospital, I felt urgency physically before I could articulate why.

2. **Resistance Signal.** The moment that matters is usually the one you want to avoid. Standing up on the plane. Fighting with doctors. Increasing marketing spend in a recession. When every part of you wants to take it easy, that's often the signal that taking it hard is exactly what's needed.

3. **Disproportionate Impact Signal.** Ask yourself, "Will the outcome of this moment affect more than just this moment? Will this conversation impact just today or the entire relationship? Will this decision affect just this quarter or the company's trajectory?" The bigger the ripple effect, the more the moment matters.

These signals are your early warning system. In part two of this book, I show you how each type of moment has its own specific signals, its own preparation requirements, its own way of showing up. But for now, let these signals be your clues that a moment is coming. Practice recognizing them in your day-to-day life. The faster you can feel a moment coming, the better prepared you'll be to meet its arrival.

The Efficiency Trap

We live in an age obsessed with optimization. Every interaction should be frictionless. Every process should be automated. Every human touchpoint that can be eliminated should be, in the name of efficiency and scale. But we're discovering something counterintuitive: the harder path often creates exponentially more value than the easy one does.

Advisors at the global management consulting firm McKinsey & Company have found that companies maintaining "inefficient" human touches see customer lifetime value increase by 23 percent.[22] These include handwritten notes instead of automated emails and calls instead of chatbots. A related *Harvard Business Review* study found that customers with even one meaningful human interaction are 75 percent more likely to remain loyal during downturns.[23]

Why? Because taking it hard creates moments that matter. It's easier to send an email than make a call. It's easier to text than meet face-to-face. It's easier to let an algorithm handle customer service than to train a human to genuinely care. But easier doesn't create the moments that transform businesses, relationships, or lives.

The companies winning aren't those with the smoothest checkout or fastest response. They're the ones creating moments that stick long after the transaction is complete. Those moments almost always require taking it hard.

This connects directly back to that plane, to those hospital rooms, to that business decision. In each case, the easier, more efficient path was available and socially acceptable. But the moments that mattered required something more.

Not All Moments Are Created Equal

I need to be honest with you. I'm sharing some of the most intense moments of my life, and they might feel overwhelming or disconnected from your daily reality. A plane losing engines. Multiple medical crises. Betting the company during a recession. These aren't typical Tuesday afternoon situations.

But that's not the point. I'm not sharing these stories because I think my moments are bigger or more important than yours. I'm sharing them because they taught me something that applies to every moment that matters, regardless of scale.

Life is built in the moments no one thinks matter. Your defining moment might happen in your kitchen tomorrow morning when your teenager storms in, angry about something, and you have to choose between the easy response ("Not now, I'm late") and the hard one (putting down your phone and asking, "What's really going on?").

It might happen in next week's team meeting when everyone's nodding along to a bad idea and you have to decide whether to be the person who speaks up or the person who stays comfortable.

It might be tonight when your partner starts telling you about their day and you choose to close your laptop completely instead of half-listening while you finish that email.

These moments don't come with warning sirens or fire trucks. They show up disguised as ordinary interactions. But they matter just as much as any emergency landing or lifesaving surgery.

The truth is that I've lived a life full of big swings. Marrying my high school sweetheart. Adopting three older kids from Russia over a span of eleven months. Starting a business with no backup plan. Some of these I chose; others chose me. The medical crises, the business challenges, the moments of terror at 35,000 feet; nobody asks for these. But we all face our own versions of them.

What I've learned is that taking it hard has nothing to do with the size of the moment and everything to do with recognizing when a moment matters more than your comfort. It could be the two-minute conversation where you choose to be truly present instead of efficient. Or the apology you offer your child when you could have just maintained authority. Or the thank-you note you write by hand when an email would be faster.

These aren't lesser moments. They're the same moments, just wearing different clothes.

The Twenty-Four-Hour Moment Audit

Before you learn to recognize all seven types of moments, try this simple exercise for the next twenty-four hours.

Start by setting three alarms on your phone: morning, afternoon, and evening. When each alarm goes off, ask yourself, "What moment just happened that someone might remember?"

Not what you accomplished. Not what you checked off your list. What moment might stick in someone's memory?

Maybe it was the way you responded when your direct report admitted a mistake. Maybe it was putting your phone completely away when your teenager asked a question over breakfast. Maybe it was taking the stairs to personally deliver that document instead of sending an email.

Once you've found your answer, ask yourself, "Did I take it easy or take it hard in that moment?"

That's it. Just notice. Don't judge. Just observe how many potential moments pass by unrecognized, how many opportunities to take it hard you let slip into taking it easy.

One executive who tried this told me, "I realized I had three moments before lunch that could have mattered, and I sleepwalked through all of them. The awareness alone changed how I showed up for the rest of the day."

This is your entry point. Start seeing the moments. Everything else builds from there.

The Revolution Begins with a Choice

Remember: the moments that define us aren't the easy ones. They're the moments when we choose to take it hard when taking it easy would be completely understandable.

The take-it-hard revolution isn't about making everything difficult for difficulty's sake. It's about developing the sensitivity to recognize which moments matter and the courage to meet them with everything we have, even when we're not sure it will be enough.

My wife could have accepted her limitations after the strokes. She could have taken the disability payments and adjusted to a smaller life. I could have trusted the first doctor's diagnosis and taken my wife home to wait until Monday. My company could have cut marketing in 2009 like every responsible company was doing, but we didn't. Each time, the easier path was right there, socially acceptable and completely understandable, yet utterly wrong for the moment we were in.

The moments that matter don't care about being easy. They don't care that you're tired, that you're scared, that you're unqualified, that you'd rather be doing literally anything else. They only care whether you show up.

Before you turn the page or hurry forward into today's next activity, I want you to sit with these questions: Where in your life are you taking it easy when you should be taking it hard? What conversation have you been avoiding because it's uncomfortable? What risk have you been postponing because failure would hurt? What advocacy have you been withholding because speaking up would make you unpopular? What change have you been resisting because the familiar, even if it's slowly killing you, feels safer than the unknown?

The thread that connects the plane, the hospital, and the business decision is this: in each case, taking it hard meant being willing to be uncomfortable, to be unpopular, to be wrong, in service of something that mattered more than my comfort. That's what I'm asking you to consider for your own life.

The revolution doesn't require you to adopt three kids or fight with doctors or bet your company. It just requires you to recognize that not all moments are created equal and the ones that matter require you to take it hard.

Even when your spouse grabs your arm and tells you you're not in charge. Even when doctors say you're being ridiculous. Even when the board thinks you're reckless. Even when the whole plane is watching and you have no idea what to do next. **Especially then.**

Because those are the moments that matter. And what you do in those moments determines not just what happens next but who you become.

The universe is conspiring in your favor. But first, you have to take it hard.

PART TWO:
THE FRAMEWORK

SEVEN MOMENTS THAT CONTROL EVERYTHING: IN BUSINESS, IN LIFE, AND IN RELATIONSHIPS

"How you do anything is
how you do everything."
MARTHA BECK

CHAPTER 4

INCEPTION MOMENTS: THE FIRST DOMINO

The glass windows in front of me were covered in calculations, scenarios, and desperate math. I stood before them, dry-erase marker in hand, blinking at any scribble that might transform into an answer before my eyes. It was 2009, the economy was in freefall, and I had forty-eight hours to figure out how to save PeopleG2 without laying off a single person.

The mortgage industry was our bread and butter, and it had completely collapsed. One client went from hiring thirty people a day to a complete recruiting freeze. It happened overnight.

I'd been writing on these windows for hours, trying every combination I could imagine to make the numbers work. Cut this, restructure that, eliminate these expenses. Nothing worked. The math was brutal and unforgiving.

Then I started dreaming differently. What if we didn't have rent? What if we didn't have phone systems? What if we eliminated the break-room costs, the office supplies, the utilities? I wasn't trying to trim fat anymore; I was imagining a completely different animal.

Our lease was up in thirty days.

That's when it hit me. We didn't need a new building. The truth is that we didn't need any building at all.

Within that forty-eight-hour window, I decided we'd go completely remote. At the time, I thought it would be temporary. Send everyone home, weather the storm, come back after things have improved. I had no idea I was creating an inception moment that would define the next twelve years of our company and save every single job.

But I also had no idea how badly I was about to screw it up.

The Inception Hiding in the Trash

Inception moments are the first dominoes in a chain reaction you can't stop once it starts. Get them right and you'll create momentum that can carry you for years. Get them wrong and you'll spend those same years trying to recover.

Author Stephen King learned this the hard way. In 1973, he hammered a nail into his bedroom wall just to hold all the rejection slips. He was teaching high school English, living in a trailer, writing at night on a typewriter balanced on his knees.

He started writing *Carrie* but gave up after a few pages. Trying to master the voice of a teenage girl felt wrong. He crumpled up those pages and threw them in the trash.[24]

But Tabitha, his wife, pulled those pages out of the wastebasket. She smoothed them out, read them, and did something

Figure 4.1. Inception moments are the first dominoes.

that changed literary history. She told him to keep going. Not tomorrow. Not when he felt inspired. She wanted him to continue right then.

"You've got something here," she averred. "I want to know what happens next."[25]

Tabitha's intervention became the real inception. She sat with him and helped him understand how teenage girls think and talk. When Doubleday then bought *Carrie* for $2,500, King thought that was the victory. The paperback rights sold for $400,000. That inception moment, pulled from a wastebasket, launched one of the most successful writing careers in history.

Sometimes inception moments hide inside what we've already dismissed as failure.

When Your Best Employee Is Actually Your Worst

Three weeks after my forty-eight-hour decision, we'd moved everyone home. No more office. No more commute. No more physical file folders that employees could grab from a basket and work through at their own pace.

That last detail seemed minor, but it absolutely wasn't.

We had an employee in our verifications department who everyone thought was our superstar. Let's call her Nancy. She got through more employment verifications per day than anyone else on the team could. She was lovely, brought in baked goods all the time, and had been with us for years. By every measure, she was a model employee.

When we went remote, we had to change from physical folders to digital ones. More importantly, we had to assign them randomly instead of letting people choose their own work. It seemed like a small operational shift, and we didn't think twice about it.

Within a week, Nancy's performance had completely cratered. She went from our best performer to our absolute worst, and we couldn't figure out what was happening. Was the technology confusing her? Was working from home just not suited to her style? We asked questions, offered support, and tried everything we could think of.

Then we looked at the data more carefully, and the truth hit us like a sledgehammer.

Nancy had been cherry-picking the easy files for years. While her colleagues struggled with complicated verifications that required multiple calls and detective work, she'd been quietly taking all the simple ones. She'd grab the large corporations with dedicated verification hotlines and the recent employment cases for which everything was readily available. She'd arrive early, take all the easy folders, and leave the difficult ones for everyone else.

Nobody had complained because she was so nice. The baked goods probably helped. But our remote inception had accidentally created a forced transparency that revealed the truth. When work was assigned randomly and everyone got the same mix of easy and difficult verifications, Nancy couldn't keep up.

She resigned within three weeks, citing the new system as the cause. We all knew the real reason, though. The writing was on the wall.

That inception moment of going remote had revealed a truth that had been hiding in plain sight for years. It made me wonder what else we were missing, what other comfortable lies we were telling ourselves because we'd never been forced to look closely.

The Disaster of Being Unprepared

Not every inception moment is planned. Some of them hit you in the face when you're absolutely not ready for them.

Oprah Winfrey discovered this on her first day as a news anchor in Baltimore. At twenty-two, she was recruited from Nashville, where she'd been the youngest news anchor and the first Black female anchor in that market. Her move to Baltimore was sure to be her next big inception moment.

But it turned out to be a disaster.

When tragic news stories trickled up her teleprompter screen, emotion seeped, palpably, through her voice. The stories clearly affected her, and the audience could tell. Management told her she was "too emotional," that she needed to be more detached.

Within eight months, they demoted her to the morning talk show. She was devastated.

But Oprah understood something that most of us miss: inception moments aren't always the ones we choose. Sometimes they choose us. That morning show, that demotion, that failure actually put her in a format where her emotional connection to stories wasn't a liability. Instead, it was her greatest asset. The empathy that made her wrong for news made her perfect for connecting with guests and audiences.[26]

"It was a demotion," she said years later. "But it felt like a homecoming."[27]

That failed inception as a news anchor became the real inception of her career. The very qualities that made her wrong for news made her perfect for what came next. *The Oprah Winfrey Show* would never have existed had she succeeded in that first role. Sometimes the worst inception moments become the best ones, but only if you're willing to see them differently.

The Mistakes That Almost Killed Us

When PeopleG2 went remote, we assumed we could replicate our in-person operations without issue. Turns out we were spectacularly wrong.

First, we thought Skype could be our phone system. Everyone would have a number, and we would transfer calls. What we didn't anticipate was the unreliability. Calls dropped constantly. Customers thought we were amateurs. We scrambled for alternatives.

Next, we had no idea how communication would actually work. In the office, information traveled through proximity. You'd overhear important conversations, bump into people with updates, and absorb knowledge through osmosis. At home, everyone was working in an information silo. We were all working hard but had absolutely no idea what anyone else was doing.

Email became completely overwhelming. Important information got buried in endless threads. Nobody knew where to find anything, and we were drowning in digital chaos.

It took us weeks to realize we needed a central communication hub. We became one of the first companies to adopt HipChat, which was later bought by Atlassian, which created Slack. We made a radical decision that surprised everyone: no more internal emails. Everything internal had to go into our chat platform. We needed one source of truth, one place for all communication.

But the biggest inception failure was that we didn't realize how lonely and disconnected people would feel. Connie, one of our top employees, had been terrified of going remote. "I won't be able to communicate with people," she told me. "I won't know what's going on, and I'm going to be completely isolated."

I assured her it would be fine. The truth is that I had no idea what I was talking about.

The Recovery That Taught Us Everything

Two weeks into our remote experiment, something unexpected happened. Connie called me. When I realized who was on the other end of the line, I thoroughly expected to receive her resignation.

"This is the best thing we've ever done!" she proclaimed instead.

I was completely confused. This was the same person who'd been terrified, who'd only agreed to try this new way of communicating because I'd insisted. What had changed?

"I can actually think now," she explained. "I can work without interruptions. I can go deep on problems without someone stopping by my desk every five minutes. I'm getting more done in six hours than I used to get done in ten."

She was half right. The deep work was definitely better. But we'd lost something crucial in the transition: the random collisions that create innovation, the casual conversations that build trust, the human moments that make work about more than just completing tasks.

I thought I could solve this with information. So I spent hours every week creating a digital newspaper called the *PeopleG2 Times*. It included updates from every department, photos from home offices, celebrations of wins, and the like.

Nobody read it. Maybe 20 percent opened it. Maybe 5 percent read past the first paragraph. I was crushed.

Then someone finally told me the truth during a one-on-one meeting. "It feels like homework," they revealed. "In the office, I'd learn this stuff naturally. I'd bump into someone getting coffee and they'd mention their project. It was quick and organic and natural. This feels like required reading that I'm supposed to complete."

They were absolutely right. I was trying to force connection through documentation, but what people needed wasn't information delivery. They needed spontaneous moments and accidental collisions. They needed the digital equivalent of hallway conversations.

So we invented new meeting types:

- **Cockroach Meetings.** Optional meetings that last about fifteen minutes and are designed to address small problems. It's like finding a cockroach in your bathroom. It's not a crisis, but you'll need help from an exterminator to deal with it.

- **Ostrich Meetings.** Meetings intended to help you get your head out of the sand about something. Admitting you don't know is the first step to learning.

- **Tiger Team Meetings.** Mandatory meetings that require heavy preparation and have specific intended outcomes, like coming face-to-face with a tiger. When something can transform or destroy you, make sure to get one of these meetings on the books.

These weren't just meetings. They were inception moments that could happen any time and be called by anyone.

The Third Space: Where Inception Lives

Every inception moment is preceded by the Third Space, that pause between what was and what will be, where you decide not just what to do but who to be when the moment arrives.

I should clarify, though, that the Third Space isn't just a pause. It's an active transformation zone where you consciously shift from who you've been into who you need to be for what's coming. Think about actors backstage before a performance. They're not just waiting around. They're actively becoming their character, breathing differently, moving differently, thinking differently. That's the Third Space in action.

When I was drawing on those glass windows with my dry-erase marker, I wasn't just doing math. I was in my Third Space, preparing myself to be a different kind of CEO. The person who'd been managing stable growth for eight years was dying, and the one who would lead through crisis was being born. Those forty-eight hours were my backstage transformation.

Every morning before meetings, I'd take five minutes in my Third Space. I wouldn't plan what to say; I would plan who I was going to be. Did the team need a confident leader today? An empathetic listener? Someone to push them forward? The Third Space let me choose consciously rather than react unconsciously.

I started teaching this concept to our employees. Before client calls, I'd tell them, "Take thirty seconds. Close your eyes, breathe, and ask yourself who this client needs you to be right now. Are they looking for a problem solver? An advisor? Someone to just listen? Don't just prepare your materials; prepare your presence."

One employee told me this changed everything for her. "I used to just jump from task to task, bringing whatever mood I was in with me. Now I reset between contexts. My client calls go better; my team meetings are more productive. I'm not just doing different things; I'm being different versions of myself for different moments."

We all have different versions of ourselves. Selecting the appropriate version to engage with in the moment ahead helps ensure that we're most able to meet that moment and use it to create successful outcomes.

The Economics of Taking It Hard

People always ask me about the return on investment, or ROI, of these inception moments. What's the business case for fortune cookies and Swedish Fish? Let me give you the real numbers.

At PeopleG2, we realized that we could create inception moments for new hires with thoughtful investment and by making a few changes. Before we redesigned onboarding, first-year turnover was 35 percent. Every departure costs roughly $15,000 in recruiting, training, and lost productivity. With forty employees, that's $210,000 annually in turnover costs.

With the redesign, we started spending about $500 per new employee to turn a simple hiring process into an inception moment. That investment covered welcome packages, proper onboarding, and my time for culture training.

The first year after implementing our inception moment design, our turnover dropped to 12 percent. We went from losing fourteen people to losing just five. That's nine fewer departures, which saved us $135,000 in year one alone.

The investment was maybe $20,000 total for all the new hires that year. The return was $135,000 in savings. That's a 675-percent ROI, and that's just from year one. It doesn't count the improved productivity from engaged employees, the referrals from employees who evangelized about their first day, or the client retention that came from lower turnover.

But the real economics go even deeper than that. An employee who has an amazing first day tells people about it. They post on LinkedIn; they become recruiters before they've even finished their first week. Our cost per hire dropped 40 percent because our employees were sending us qualified candidates. "You have to work here," they'd say. "Let me tell you about my first day."

Creating Inception Moments by Design

The secret to our success was learning how to intentionally create inception moments. The key was in recognizing that first days, first meetings, and first impressions carry disproportionate weight in memory and impact.

The science behind this idea is brutal. Princeton researchers Janine Willis and Alexander Todorov showed participants photographs of faces for different lengths of time: 100 milliseconds, 500 milliseconds, a full second. Then they asked for ratings on trustworthiness and competence.

Judgments made after 100 milliseconds correlated almost perfectly with judgments made given unlimited time. Additional time didn't change the verdict. It only increased confidence.[28]

We decide how we feel about others in one-tenth of a second. Less time than it takes to blink. And we stick by those feelings.

By the time a new employee has walked from the lobby to their desk, hundreds of micro-judgments have already been made. By the time a client has finished shaking your hand, their impression is essentially locked. Everything after that first moment isn't forming the impression. It's confirming or defending against what's already been decided.

This is why our old onboarding approach was so catastrophically wrong. In that old system, new employees would spend their first day drowning in paperwork, sitting alone at a desk, wondering if they'd made the right choice. We'd hand them a stack of forms, point them to their workspace, and hope for the best. Sometimes their computer wouldn't be ready. Sometimes their business cards wouldn't arrive for weeks. Sometimes they wouldn't even meet their manager on their first day.

We were wasting the most important moment in the entire employee life cycle: the day when they're most excited, most impressionable, most ready to believe in what we're building.

We flipped everything around. We sent all the paperwork in advance so they could complete it on their own time, and we paid them for that time. Their first day, we realized, should be about connection, not compliance.

But let's back up. Even before their first day, new hires would receive a package at their home. Company swag, yes, but also something personal. During the interview process, we'd ask casual questions about their favorite snacks, how they took their coffee, little preferences that showed we were paying attention. One person mentioned loving Swedish Fish during their interview. Guess what was waiting in their welcome package?

Sometimes we'd send a giant fortune cookie with a custom message inside, something specific to their role, their journey, their story. These weren't throwaway items. They were the kinds of things people kept on their desks because they mattered.

Within the first two days, every new employee had a thirty-minute culture training session with me personally. Not with HR, not with their manager, but with the CEO. I'd explain how we really operated, what actually mattered, how our weird meeting names worked. But most importantly, I'd tell them something crucial.

"I need you to be my eyes and ears," I'd explain. "If what you see happening doesn't match what I'm telling you right now, I need to know immediately. If someone says you can't do something that I just said you could do, tell me right away. You're seeing our company with fresh eyes, and that's invaluable to me."

The ripple effects were incredible.

When someone's first day is amazing, they tell people about it. They post about it on social media. They become recruiters before they've even finished their first week. One employee told me years later that she'd never forgotten her welcome package, that it made her feel like she mattered before she'd done a single minute of work for us.

Testing Trust from Day One

New clients taught me something fascinating about inception moments. They don't trust you on day one, and why would they? You're new, you're unproven, and you're making the same promises that every other vendor made before disappointing them.

They would test us. Almost every new client would send us past searches they knew were problematic, often background checks completed by previous vendors who had missed something important. They wanted to see if we'd find what others hadn't.

Because we ran our expanded Southern California criminal search, checking multiple counties instead of just one, we almost always found more than the previous vendors had. That could be an assault charge in the next county over, a DUI from a weekend trip, or discrepancies that crossed county lines.

One client sent us five test cases. Their previous vendor had found issues in two of them. We found issues in four. When the client called me after receiving their results, I could hear the suspicion in their voice.

"These are test cases, aren't they?" I asked.

There was silence on the line, then, "How did you know?"

"Because good clients test new vendors. You should test us. And we just passed, didn't we?"

That inception moment, calling out their test, acknowledging it, and celebrating that they were smart enough to test us completely changed the entire relationship. We went from being just another vendor to being a real partner in one conversation. They knew we saw them as sophisticated buyers, not just another account.

Fear and Excitement: The Same Chemical

During our remote transition, I was terrified. I couldn't sleep. My heart raced. My stomach was in knots.

Then I ran into some research that calmed me. Fear and excitement, it showed, create nearly identical physiological responses. The same adrenaline, the same cortisol, the same elevated heart rate. Your body cannot tell the difference.[29]

The only difference is the story you tell yourself about how you're feeling and why.

So I started reframing. Every time I felt afraid, I'd say out loud, "I'm not scared; I'm excited." It sounds ridiculous, but it worked.

I started teaching this reframing technique to the team, especially during inception moments when the stakes felt highest. When a new employee was nervous about their first day, I'd tell them, "You're not nervous; you're excited to contribute." When a client was anxious about switching vendors, I'd reframe it: "You're not worried; you're energized about getting better results."

One employee told me this completely changed her career: "I used to avoid anything that made me nervous. Now I seek it out because I know that nervous means important. If I'm not a little scared, the moment probably doesn't matter enough."

Remember those physical signs we discussed in chapter 3? The ones that help you recognize moments as they're happening? Recognizing your sweaty palms or fluttering pulse as indicators that you're approaching a moment, and reimagining those indicators as excitement rather than fear, can help you harness your power and step into that moment with confidence.

Taking It Hard in the Beginning

The difference between taking it easy and taking it hard is most visible during inception moments. When you take it easy with onboarding, you send the paperwork, assign a desk, and hope it works out. When you take it hard, you create an experience they'll talk about for years.

When Stephen King's wife pulled those pages from the trash, she wasn't taking it easy. She could have let him quit, avoided the difficult conversation, and saved herself from the potential pushback. Instead, she took it hard. She fought for those pages, for that story, for the writer she knew he could become.

When Oprah got demoted from news anchor, she could have taken it easy. She could have quit, found another news job, kept trying to be what they wanted her to be. Instead, she took it hard. She embraced what felt like failure and turned it into the inception of something entirely new.

Your Inception Moment Audit

For the next week, I want you to track every beginning in your organization. Every first meeting with a client, every employee's first day, every project kickoff, every new initiative launch.

Ask yourself these questions: "Did we treat this like an inception moment or just another task? Did the person experiencing it feel like it mattered? Will they remember this a year from now? What story will they tell about this beginning?"

Then pick one, just one, and redesign it completely. Make it remarkable. Make it worth talking about. Make it an inception moment that creates the momentum you want.

What I learned with those markers on glass in 2009 is that sometimes the best inception moments come from the worst situations. Sometimes failure is just the first draft of success. Sometimes the thing you throw in the trash is exactly what someone else needs to pull out and smooth straight.

But you have to be willing to take it hard. You have to be willing to cover your windows with desperate math, to admit you don't know what you're doing, to send giant fortune cookies and Swedish Fish. You have to be willing to create meetings called "Cockroach" and "Ostrich" and "Tiger Team." You have to believe that how you begin determines everything that follows.

The universe is conspiring in your favor, but it starts with inception. And inception starts with recognizing that not all beginnings are created equal.

Some beginnings are worth taking hard.

For downloadable onboarding checklists and inception moment design templates, visit chrisdyer.com/moments.

"In the space between
chaos and shape, there
was another chance."
JEANETTE WINTERSON

CHAPTER 5

TRANSITION MOMENTS: THE SPACE BETWEEN TRAPEZES

The tennis shoes should have been my first clue.

I was standing at the summit of Mount Kilimanjaro, nearly 20,000 feet above sea level, my hand pressed against the weathered wooden sign that marked the achievement. Uhuru Peak. The roof of Africa. It was July 2023. I'd trained for an entire year for this moment, spent thousands of dollars on gear, flown halfway around the world, and climbed for eight grueling days to reach this spot. This was it. The goal. The dream. The thing.

"Finally! I've done it!"

The euphoria lasted maybe ten minutes. Long enough for photos, for the obligatory celebration, for the acknowledgment that yes, I'd actually made it. Then I noticed the guides doing something odd. They were sitting on rocks, unlacing their heavy hiking boots, pulling out tennis shoes from their packs. Not fancy trail runners or technical approach shoes. Regular tennis shoes. The kind you'd wear to the grocery store.

"What are you doing?" I asked.

"Getting ready for the real work," one of them replied, not even looking up from his laces.

I'd spent a year preparing to go up. Hundreds of training hikes. Every session focused on the ascent. When you're hiking locally, going down feels like an afterthought. The easy part.

What nobody told me was that going down would be the hardest physical challenge of my life.

It took two and a half days to descend. The entire way down, my knees were screaming, my quads burning, and my toes jamming into my boots with every step. The path was so steep in places that I had to do a sideways shuffle, using trekking poles like crutches.

By the end of the first day going down, I would have gladly spent another eight days climbing up instead. My hiking boots, perfect for the ascent, were now instruments of torture. The guides in their tennis shoes seemed to float while I stumbled and cursed.

I had the wrong goal. The goal wasn't to reach the top of the mountain. The goal was to finish the entire journey safely. But I'd been so focused on the summit, so fixated on that wooden sign, that I'd completely missed preparing for what was to come after. There was power in the transition: from going up to going down, from achieving to completing, from conquering to surviving.

The Parallel I Couldn't Ignore

Eighteen months earlier, I'd reached a different kind of summit. On December 31, 2021, I stepped outside a New Year's Eve dinner to sign the final documents transferring ownership of the company I'd built over twenty years. Another goal achieved. Another mountain climbed.

The sale was good for everyone. My employees got bonuses, job security with a larger company, and better benefits. I got financial freedom and the validation that comes from a successful exit. Summit reached. Sign touched. Goal achieved.

What I didn't understand was that selling your company is like reaching the top of Kilimanjaro. The achievement is just the halfway point. The real challenge is navigating who you become when your identity has been tied to something for two decades that's suddenly not yours anymore.

For twenty years, I was Chris Dyer, CEO. That's how I introduced myself. That's how others knew me. That's where my purpose lived. Then one day, I wasn't. And just like on Kilimanjaro, I was completely unprepared for the descent.

The months after the sale were brutal in ways I'd never anticipated. I'd wake up with ideas for the company and realize I had no company. I'd see problems in the business world and start planning solutions, only to remember that I had no team to execute them with. I'd built my entire life around being a leader, a builder, an entrepreneur, and suddenly I was just a guy with money in the bank and no idea what would come next.

Nobody tells you about the identity crisis that comes after you sell. They congratulate you on the exit, ask about the terms, and assume you're living the dream. They don't ask about the 3 AM panic attacks when you wonder if you'll ever build anything meaningful again. They don't mention the strange grief of seeing your company's website with someone else's name as CEO. They don't warn you that the transition from founder to former founder can be harder than building the company in the first place.

Mandela's Eighteen-Year Third Space

Understanding transitions as the real work became easier when I studied Nelson Mandela. Most people know he spent twenty-seven years in prison. What they don't understand is that he used those years as the ultimate transition preparation.

He learned Afrikaans in secret, not because he loved the language of his oppressors but because transition requires understanding the people you're transitioning with. He studied his guards' lives, learned their children's names. He wasn't killing time. He was preparing for a moment that might never come.

That's right. Mandela spent eighteen years preparing for a transition that was never guaranteed. Most of us can't prepare for transitions we know are coming next month.

When he was finally released in 1990, the world expected revenge. After all, he'd endured nearly three decades of imprisonment. His mother and son had died while he was locked away. Mandela had every right to demand retribution.

Instead, he hired his former prison guards as part of his presidential security detail.[30] The very people who had controlled his every movement for decades were now protecting him as president. The world gasped. His own party questioned his sanity. But Mandela understood something about transitions: the space between what was and what will be is where transformation actually happens.

Those guards became some of his most loyal protectors.[31] They knew him in ways his political allies never could. They'd watched him for eighteen years, seen him choose dignity over bitterness day after day, witnessed his commitment to something larger than personal vindication. The transition from guard to protector, from oppressor to ally, was possible because Mandela had spent so many years preparing for it.

The Military Spouse Revelation

I discovered how brutal transitions could be through an unexpected source: military spouses. We'd hired Sarah as a customer service representative, and she was exceptional. Then her husband got orders to transfer from California to Virginia, and she scheduled a call to give notice.

"I'm sorry," she professed during a video call, the defeat in her voice echoing in my speakers. "This is the third job I've had to leave in six years. I'm tired of starting over."

Military families know transitions better than anyone does. Every few years, and sometimes more frequently, they pack up their entire lives and start fresh. New state, new schools, new friends, new everything. The service member has continuity through their military role, but their spouses face complete life disruption with each move.

"What if you didn't have to quit?" I inquired.

Sarah looked confused. We were a remote company by then, had been since 2009, but she assumed that moving across the country meant leaving the job. That's what had always happened before.

"Keep working for us," I said. "Take a month to handle the move. Full pay, don't touch your PTO. When you're settled in Virginia, log back in and keep doing what you're doing."

She stared at me through the screen like I was speaking a foreign language. "Full pay, while I'm moving?"

"Moving is hard enough without losing income. Plus, you're going to be dealing with everything: finding housing, registering cars, getting kids in school, finding new doctors. That's work. Hard work. We'll support you through it," I offered.

What started as a one-off decision became formal policy. Any employee dealing with a military relocation got full pay during their transition month, without impacting their PTO. Instead of, "When will you be back online?" we asked, "What do you need during this transition?"

The ROI was incredible. Sarah became our biggest evangelist with other military families. We started getting applications from military spouses specifically because they'd heard we understood transitions. Our retention rate for military families was 94 percent, compared with the 60-percent industry average.

One military spouse wrote me a letter that I still have to this day. "Every other company treated our moves like I was abandoning them," it reads. "You treated it like we were going through something together. I've never forgotten that during the hardest transition of my life, my company was my stability."

Transitions can be devastating, but they can also be an opportunity to create moments that matter for the people who matter, in your company and in your life.

The Space Between Trapezes

The best metaphor for transitions comes from Danaan Parry in his writing on trapeze artists.[32] One might easily assume the moment of glory is when the artist catches the second bar. But the real moment is the space between letting go of the first bar and grasping the second, that breathless time when the artist is flying through space with empty hands.

Most of us clutch the first bar even when it's not taking us where we want to go. Others grab for the new bar too early and fall. Transformation happens in that terrifying space between, when you're holding nothing but still moving forward.

This concept became real for me watching others navigate major life transitions. In one case, a friend's teenage daughter struggled immensely when the family moved cross-country during her junior year of high school. They'd prepared for the logistics of the move, researched the new school, even visited

Figure 5.1. The space between trapezes.

beforehand. But nobody had prepared her for the identity transition she'd undergo. Where once she'd been someone with deep roots and established friendships, she'd suddenly become the unknown new kid trying to find her place. And that was tough.

Her parents initially saw her struggles as teenage rebellion. The usual symptoms appeared: poor grades, isolation, anger. But when they reframed it as a transition challenge rather than a behavior problem, everything shifted. They stopped punishing and started supporting. They acknowledged how hard it was to be between identities, to have let go of whom she was but not yet grabbed hold of whom she could become.

The Trust Transfer Equation

I certainly felt that way when I sold my company and lost the title I'd built my identity around. It was through that transition and through witnessing the transitions of others in my life that I discovered a pattern. I call it the Trust Transfer Equation:

Vulnerability × Presence × Consistency = Safe Passage

Surviving difficult transitions and coming out the other side requires three crucial components:

- **Vulnerability** means admitting you don't know how to navigate this transition. When Mandela was released, he could have pretended to have all the answers. Instead, he admitted he needed to learn about a world that had changed dramatically. That vulnerability made others want to help him succeed.

- **Presence** means being fully in the transition, not trying to skip ahead. On Kilimanjaro, I was so focused on the summit that I missed the signs that the descent would require different preparation. Presence means feeling discomfort without trying to escape it.

- **Consistency** means showing up the same way every day, even when progress feels impossible. After selling my company, there were days I wanted to hide. But I kept showing up to networking events and kept exploring what might come next. Consistency builds the bridge to whatever comes after.

Miss any one element and the equation falls apart.

Attack Behaviors, Not People

Through years of managing people in transition, I've learned something crucial about navigating the stress and resistance that come with change. When someone is struggling through a transition and acting out, you have to separate their temporary behavior from their permanent value as a person.

The principle is simple but powerful: address what they're doing, not who they are. The behavior is temporary, a symptom of the transition stress. The person is permanent, worthy of respect regardless of their current struggle.

One of the best salespeople I knew, let's call him Marcus, became incredibly negative during his company's shift to remote work. Every team meeting, he'd complain about the technology, about missing the office energy, about how this would never work. Other employees started avoiding calls with him.

The instinct is to label Marcus as toxic. Marcus is resistant to change. Marcus is bringing everyone down. But attacking the person rather than the behavior never works, especially during transitions.

So his manager called him, not to reprimand but to understand.

"Marcus, I've noticed you're struggling with the remote transition. The negativity in meetings isn't like you. What's really going on?"

The floodgates opened. His marriage was struggling because now he was home all day in a tense environment he used to escape by going to the office. His teenage son was also doing school from home, and they were constantly clashing. He felt like he was failing at work and at home simultaneously.

"I hate who I'm becoming," he admitted.

"You're not becoming anyone," his manager reassured him. "You're behaving in a way that reflects your struggle with this transition. The behavior needs to change, but you're still the same valuable person and employee you've always been."

They worked together on solutions. Marcus became one of their strongest remote employees and eventually helped other struggling team members with their transitions. But it only worked because his manager attacked his behavior rather than him as a person.

The Vulnerability Window

Every transition has what I call the Vulnerability Window: the first thirty days when everything feels wrong and nothing makes sense. This is when most people give up or convince themselves that the transition was a mistake.

During those first thirty days after selling my company, I almost made three terrible decisions just to escape my discomfort. First, I nearly bought another company I didn't actually want. Then, I almost accepted a CEO position at a company whose values I didn't share. And then I came close to starting a venture in an industry I didn't understand.

The Vulnerability Window is when your judgment is most impaired but you most need good judgment. Often, the good judgment is not to rush your transition period and skip ahead into a future that you're not prepared for or that's not right for you.

Vulnerability is such a hard feeling to sit with. Many of us, me included, will do almost anything to feel like we're back in control of a situation or of ourselves or of our lives. I was a CEO, and then I was no one. Rather than diving into that hurt and doing the difficult work of interrogating why I felt insufficient without my work, how I'd let my job become my selfhood, and who I wanted to become now that I was free of that, I could simply step into a suitably similar alternative identity: business owner, CEO, founder. It would have been easy, and, for the moment at least, it would have felt good. The familiar will always be most comfortable, but it's those pesky, uncomfortable transitions that generate transformation.

What saved me was something I learned from those Kilimanjaro guides with their tennis shoes. They knew something I didn't: different phases of the journey require different equipment, different strategies, different energy. They weren't just prepared for the summit; they were prepared for every transition along the way. With a little thought and effort, I could be too.

Creating Transition Rituals

The most successful transitions I've witnessed include deliberate rituals that mark the passage from one state to another. Without rituals, transitions feel like abandonment. With them, they feel like evolution.

Pixar Animation Studios has a powerful tradition for when films wrap production. They hold what they call "Notes Day," where the entire company shuts down regular work to reflect on what they learned from a project. It's not a celebration of completion but rather an acknowledgment of transition. What worked? What didn't? What will we carry forward? What will we leave behind?

Ed Catmull, Pixar's cofounder, describes this ritual as essential to the company's creative process.[33] It transforms the end of one project into the beginning of the next. People don't just finish; they graduate. The ritual creates a bridge between what was and what will be, making the transition feel intentional rather than accidental.

After selling my company, I created my own personal ritual to mark the transition. Every morning for ninety days, I wrote three pages by hand about who I was becoming. Not who I had been as a CEO, not who I would be eventually, but who I was in that exact moment of transition. It was messy, repetitive, often incoherent. But it kept me present in the transition rather than trying to escape it.

On day ninety-one, I read all those pages back. The evolution was stunning. Day one was all grief and fear. Day thirty was confusion and possibility. Day sixty was clarity emerging. Day ninety was excitement about what was to come next. Without that ritual, I would have missed my own transformation.

The Lost Group Therapy

What nobody tells you about major professional transitions is that you lose more than a title or a role. You lose your thinking partners, your sounding board, your professional family. For twenty years, my senior team and I had been in what I now realize was essentially group therapy disguised as leadership meetings.

We talked about everything. Not just conversion rates and cash flow but also marriages that were struggling, teenagers who were rebelling, aging parents who needed care. We created space for the whole person, not just the employee persona.

When the company sold, I didn't just lose my daily responsibilities. I lost that circle of trust. The habits were still there: opening my laptop at 6 AM to check reports that were no longer mine, reaching for my phone to text my COO about a strategic insight for a strategy I no longer owned.

The new company needed me for a while, during the transition. But gradually, systematically, they learned what they needed to know. They created their own processes, built their own relationships, developed their own ways of doing things. I went from essential to helpful to optional to unnecessary.

That should have felt like success. I'd built something that could thrive without me. Instead, it felt like erasure. And, later, it felt like loss.

The Practice, Not Perfection

I need to tell you something important: I still miss transitions. Even after writing about them, teaching about them, building an entire framework around them, I still miss them.

Recently, I watched a colleague struggle through a major career pivot. She'd been a successful marketing executive for fifteen years, then decided to become a therapist. Everyone focused on either congratulating her brave decision or questioning her sanity for leaving such a lucrative career. Nobody acknowledged the brutal transition space she was occupying: too experienced to feel like a student, too inexperienced to feel competent, caught between who she'd been and who she was becoming.

It took me three months to recognize what I was seeing. Three months before, I thought to reach out and say, "This transition must be incredibly hard. You're not who you were, but you're not yet who you're becoming. That space between must feel impossible some days."

When she received my message, she called me crying. "Nobody else sees it," she revealed. "Everyone either wants me to be the executive I was or the therapist I'm becoming. Nobody acknowledges that right now I'm neither and both."

This is what I mean when I say recognizing moments is a practice, not a skill you'll ever perfect. You'll miss transitions even when you're looking for them. You'll rush through them even when you know better. But every time you catch yourself, every time you recognize a transition even if it's halfway through, you get better at it.

Your Transition Tool Kit

Based on everything I've learned from my own failures and eventual successes with transitions, I've developed a tool kit that actually works. Here are the principles you can apply the next time you find yourself in a period of transition or want to help someone you know through theirs:

- **The Vulnerability Window Protocol.** The first thirty days of any transition are the hardest. During that window, triple your presence. Remember that this stage isn't permanent, but during that vulnerability window, everything is raw and formative. Stay aware during this stage and note what you're experiencing. Allow yourself to sit with discomfort, even when you'd rather do anything else.

- **The Behavior Mirror.** When someone's behavior changes during a transition, mirror back what you see without judgment. Make observations like, "I've noticed you've been quieter in meetings since your promotion. What's that about?" The mirror reflects behavior without attacking the person, and it creates space for the transitioner to talk openly about their experience. Listen for ways you can support them during this change.

- **The Story Harvest.** Every transition contains multiple stories worth telling. Ask people in transition, "What story from this experience will you tell five years from now?" Listen for aspects you can celebrate or places where they may need additional support to turn a challenging experience into an empowering one.

- **Future-Casting Fridays.** Every Friday, spend fifteen minutes asking, "What transitions are coming that we're not seeing?" You can't prepare for everything, but you can prepare for more than you think. Seeking outside perspectives can alert you to issues you might not have realized existed otherwise.

The Summit Is Just Halfway

As I write this, I'm two years past selling my company, six months past Kilimanjaro, and probably in three transitions I haven't identified yet. But I know something now that I didn't know standing on that mountain summit, thinking I'd accomplished the goal.

The summit is just halfway. Always.

Whatever mountain you're climbing right now, whatever achievement you're pushing toward, remember that reaching it is just the beginning of the transition that follows. The real work isn't getting there; it's navigating what comes next.

Watch for the people changing into tennis shoes. They know something you need to learn. They understand that different parts of the journey require different tools, different energy, different preparation.

Your transition moments are coming. The question isn't whether you'll face them but whether you'll recognize them. Whether you'll give them the weight they deserve. Whether you'll show up fully in the space between trapezes.

Just remember to bring the right shoes.

"In any moment of decision, the best thing you can do is the right thing, the next best thing is the wrong thing, and the worst thing you can do is nothing."

THEODORE ROOSEVELT

CHAPTER 6

DECISION MOMENTS: THE POINT OF NO RETURN

The phone call came at 2 AM. It was a Tuesday morning in 1960. Martin Luther King Jr. had been arrested at a sit-in at Rich's department store in Atlanta. But unlike previous arrests, the judge had denied bail and sentenced King to four months of hard labor at Georgia State Prison. Coretta Scott King, six months pregnant, was terrified her husband wouldn't survive.

Would-be president John F. Kennedy's advisors were in full panic. The election was two weeks away. Every strategist was screaming the same thing: "Stay away from this!" Supporting King would cost Kennedy the South, and without the South, he'd lose the presidency.

The math was brutal: in 1960, supporting civil rights meant political suicide for a Democratic candidate. The Southern Democrats controlled huge swaths of the electoral map. One wrong move on race would hand Nixon the White House.

But there was Sargent Shriver, Kennedy's brother-in-law, standing in a hotel room at 2 AM. He wasn't thinking about electoral votes. He was thinking about a pregnant woman whose husband might die in prison for sitting at a lunch counter.

"Make the call," Shriver said to Kennedy. "Just call Mrs. King. Tell her you're thinking of her."

The room erupted. From every corner came the voices of campaign staff shouting Shriver down. This would destroy everything they'd worked for. The timing couldn't be worse. The risk was insane.

Kennedy sat there for a long moment, weighing everything: his entire political future balanced against one phone call to a scared pregnant woman. Then he picked up the phone.[34]

The call lasted two minutes. Kennedy simply told Coretta that he was thinking of her and her family, that he knew this must be a difficult time. That was it, no promises, no grand statements, just human compassion in the middle of a long, dark night.

Meanwhile, Robert Kennedy, JFK's brother and campaign manager, was having his own decision moment. Without telling brother John, he called the Georgia judge directly, an act that qualified as a federal intervention in a state matter and an unthinkable breach of protocol. Bobby Kennedy suggested, carefully but firmly, that King deserved bail. The judge, shocked by the call, released King the next day.

When word got out, Kennedy's advisors watched in horror as Southern newspapers erupted. The campaign was over, they thought.

But something unexpected happened. Black churches across America began distributing a pamphlet titled "The Case of Martin Luther King," which described Kennedy's calls and Nixon's silence. Two million copies circulated in the final days leading up to the election. King's father, who had previously endorsed Nixon, publicly switched his support.

Kennedy won the popular vote by 0.2 percent. In key states such as Michigan and Illinois, the Black vote had made the difference. Those two phone calls, those two minutes of decision-making against all political advice, changed American history.[35]

Decision moments aren't just about choosing between options. They're about choosing who you are when everything screams at you to be someone safer.

Figure 6.1. The point of no return.

The One-Hundred-Million-Dollar Gamble That Saved Everything

Twenty-two years later, another 2 AM phone call pierced the placid night. James Burke, CEO of Johnson & Johnson, got the call that would define his legacy. Seven people in Chicago were dead after taking Extra-Strength Tylenol capsules that someone had laced with cyanide.

The FBI told Burke this was a localized incident. The contaminated bottles came from different factories, which meant tampering happened at the retail level, not manufacturing. From a legal standpoint, Johnson & Johnson had no liability.

Burke's executives laid out the obvious path: recall the batches from Chicago stores, cooperate with the investigation, and express sympathy while maintaining that this was a criminal act beyond their control. Maybe they'd strengthen tamper-evident packaging going forward. The lawyers agreed this was the defensible position. The financial team ran the numbers on a limited recall, and it was manageable.

But Burke kept thinking about the Johnson & Johnson Credo, a one-page document written by Robert Wood Johnson in 1943 that outlined the company's mission to put customers first, before shareholders. It was literally carved in stone at their headquarters. Every executive had to sign it. But was it real or just corporate decoration?[36]

"How much would it cost to recall everything?" Burke asked. "Every single Tylenol product nationwide?"

The room went silent. Someone finally replied, "About a hundred million dollars."

This was 1982 money. Adjusted for inflation, that's over $300 million today. That was just the recall cost, not including the brand damage, the lost sales, or the market share competitors would grab. Tylenol was Johnson & Johnson's most profitable product, accounting for 17 percent of the company's income. A total recall might kill the brand entirely.

Burke made the decision that every business school still teaches: he recalled everything. Thirty-one million bottles went off the shelves nationwide, not just in Chicago, not just Extra-Strength, not just capsules, but everything with the Tylenol name.

Then he did something even more radical. He went on television and told Americans not to use any Tylenol products until further notice. Imagine a CEO telling customers not to use his company's best-selling product. The marketing team thought he'd lost his mind.[37]

Wall Street agreed. Johnson & Johnson stock plummeted. Analysts declared Tylenol dead as a brand. Who would ever trust medicine from a company associated with cyanide murders? Marketing experts said the name was too tainted to recover. Board members privately questioned if Burke should remain CEO.

But Burke wasn't done. He promised that Tylenol would return in tamper-proof packaging, something that didn't exist yet. His engineers had six weeks to invent what would become the modern safety seal, the one you still peel off every bottle today.

When Tylenol returned to shelves ten weeks later, Burke made another decision everyone advised against. Instead of quietly restocking and hoping people would forget, he launched a massive communication campaign. He appeared on *60 Minutes* and *The Phil Donahue Show*, not to spin but to be transparent about everything the company had done and why. He offered eighty million coupons for free Tylenol products to win back trust.[38]

Within a year, Tylenol had regained 92 percent of its market share. Within two years, it was more profitable than before the crisis. The *Harvard Business Review* called it "the greatest comeback in business history."[39]

But what really mattered is what happened in corporate boardrooms across America. Every CEO suddenly understood that in a crisis, the decision isn't between right and wrong. It's between short-term preservation and long-term trust. Burke had proven that choosing trust, even when it could cost everything, pays off exponentially.

The Underground Railroad's Ultimate Decision Tool

Harriet Tubman understood decision moments in a way that makes our modern challenges look trivial. Between 1850 and 1860, she made nineteen trips into the South to lead enslaved people to freedom and never lost a single person.[40] Her perfect record came from understanding a brutal truth about decision moments: sometimes there is no good option, only necessary ones.

Tubman carried a gun on every rescue mission, but not for the reason you might think. The greatest danger wasn't slave catchers or bloodhounds. It was the moment when someone in her group would panic and want to turn back.

"Dead folks tell no tales," she would announce, pointing the gun at anyone ready to flee.

The conventional telling makes Tubman sound harsh. But she understood something about decision moments under extreme pressure. If even one person turned back, they wouldn't just risk their own recapture. Under torture, they would likely reveal the entire route, the safe houses, the names of everyone who helped. One person's panic could destroy the entire network.

She carried the gun not because she wanted to use it but because its presence transformed the decision landscape. When going back meant certain death, going forward became the only option. The gun removed the paralysis of choice.

"I never ran my train off the track," Tubman boasted later, "and I never lost a passenger."[41]

What's noteworthy is that she never had to shoot anyone. The gun was what psychologists now call a "commitment device": something that makes reversal so costly that forward movement becomes inevitable. Modern behavioral economists study this principle, yet Tubman was practicing it with life-and-death stakes when psychology wasn't even a field yet.

One night in Maryland, a man in her group completely broke down. They were hiding in a swamp, surrounded by search parties with dogs. He started crying, saying he'd rather die than take another step. The others began to panic, the contagion of fear spreading through the group.

Tubman pulled out the gun. "You go on or die," she advised simply.

The man looked at the gun, then at the swamp, then at the faces of the children in their group. Something shifted in his eyes. He stood up and kept walking. Two days later, he crossed into Pennsylvania, free for the first time in his life. He later became a conductor on the Underground Railroad himself, helping others find freedom.

The gun wasn't about violence. It was about crystallizing the decision moment, removing the fog of fear that makes people forget what they're choosing between. When the options became stark, slavery or freedom, backward or forward, the right choice became obvious, even if the path remained terrifying.

The Three-Second Window

Every decision moment has what I call the Three-Second Window. It's that brief pause between stimulus and response when you choose who you're going to be. Kennedy had it when Shriver suggested calling Mrs. King. Burke had it when he heard the recall number. Tubman created it with her gun.

In those three seconds, your body tells you everything you need to know. The sweaty palms, the elevated heart rate, the tightness in your chest aren't signs of fear. They're signals that you're standing at a point of no return.

I've learned to recognize these physical signals as decision landmarks. When everything in my body activates like that, I know I'm not facing a normal choice. I'm facing a decision moment that will ripple far beyond the immediate consequences.

The mistake most of us make is trying to think our way through these moments. We list pros and cons, run scenarios, seek more data. But decision moments aren't analytical problems. They're identity problems. The question isn't, "What should I do?" It's, "Who am I?"

The Third Space Before the Point of No Return

In chapter 3, I introduced the Third Space: that deliberate pause between contexts when you prepare yourself for what's coming. Decision moments require a specific kind of Third Space preparation.

Before entering a decision moment, you need to regulate your nervous system, not to calm down but to tune up. This isn't about reducing stress. It's about channeling it. The heightened state your body enters when facing a big decision isn't a problem to solve. It's information to process.

I now have a ritual I go through before making any major decision. I take five minutes alone, close my eyes, and ask myself three questions:

1. What would I do if I knew I couldn't fail?

2. What would I do if everyone were watching?

3. What would I do if no one would ever know?

The first question reveals my actual desire. The second reveals my values. The third reveals my integrity. When all three answers point in the same direction, the decision becomes clear, even if the path remains difficult.

Kennedy's call to Coretta Scott King aligned all three. He wanted to show compassion (desire), he believed in human dignity (values), and he would have made the call even in secret (integrity). The political calculations were just noise around a clear signal.

The 10-10-10 Rule

Business journalist Suzy Welch developed a framework I've found invaluable. She calls it 10-10-10, and it consists of a three-part question: How will I feel about this decision in ten minutes, ten months, and ten years?

Most of our anxiety lives in the ten-minute window. Kennedy's advisors were living in the ten-minute fear of losing Southern votes. Johnson & Johnson's board was trapped in the ten-minute terror of hundred-million-dollar losses.

The ten-month window is where we start to see patterns. That's where Kennedy would either be president or not, where Tylenol would either be dead or recovering.

But the ten-year window is where decision moments reveal their true weight. In ten years, Kennedy's call would be seen as a defining moment in civil rights history. Johnson & Johnson's recall would become the gold standard for crisis management.

The problem is that we make most decisions based on the ten-minute window and almost never think about the ten-year legacy. Yet that legacy is where our reputations, our relationships, and our character take shape. When you're standing at a crossroads, pause long enough to ask all three questions. Let the ten-minute window inform you, let the ten-month window steady you, but let the ten-year window lead you. That's where clarity and courage usually live.

When Analysis Becomes Paralysis

The more data you gather, the harder decision moments become. This seems counterintuitive. Shouldn't more information lead to better decisions?

A study from Columbia Business School offers us some insight into this problem. Researchers set up a jam-tasting booth at a grocery store. When they offered store patrons twenty-four jam varieties, 60 percent of customers stopped to taste, but only 3 percent bought any jam. When they reduced their selection to six varieties, only 40 percent stopped, but 30 percent made a purchase. That's ten times more purchases with fewer options.[42]

Apple understood this principle when they shifted their iPhone lineup strategy. For years, the company had been expanding their range, offering multiple models at different price points. But they discovered something counterintuitive: when they simplified from offering three distinct choices to primarily featuring two clear options, their flagship model and their standard model, sales actually increased. The paradox of choice was costing Apple customers who were paralyzed by trying to optimize their purchase decision. By reducing options, the company made the decision easier and drove more sales, proving that even in technology, where we assume more choice is always better, constraint can be more powerful than variety.[43]

Decision moments work the same way. The more options you analyze, the more paralyzed you become. Not because you can't choose but because you're trying to optimize instead of decide.

Optimization is about finding the best possible outcome. Decision is about choosing a path and committing to it. They're fundamentally different mental operations. When Kennedy called Mrs. King, he wasn't optimizing for electoral success. When Burke recalled all Tylenol products, he wasn't optimizing for quarterly earnings.

They were both deciding who they wanted to be.

The Decision Story

After every major decision, I now do something that seems simple but has proven invaluable: I write down why I made that choice. Not what I decided but why. The story behind the decision.

This isn't for accountability or documentation. It's because decision moments shape us, and if we don't capture the shaping while it's happening, we lose the lesson.

Johnson & Johnson still has Burke's notes from the Tylenol crisis. In them, he wrote, "The Credo is either real or it's decoration. Today, we find out which." That's not a business justification. It's an identity declaration.

Years later, when Burke was asked about that hundred-million-dollar decision, he could point to those notes and admit, "We didn't make a financial decision. We made a values decision. The Credo said customers come first, and we proved we meant it." That story, that why, became more valuable than any financial return. It transformed Johnson & Johnson from a company that sold medicine into a company people trusted with their lives.

Every company faces decision moments that test their stated values. The ones that write down their why, that document the story behind the decision, create a mythology that guides future choices. Burke's decision story became the template for how Johnson & Johnson has handled every crisis since. When faced with difficult choices, employees ask, "What would Burke do? What does the Credo demand?" The story of the decision became more powerful than any policy manual could ever be.

Your Decision Moment Audit

Before you face your next decision moment, you need to know where you typically fail. In my work with hundreds of leaders, I've found three common failure points:

- **Identification Failure.** You treat all decisions equally. The decision about lunch carries the same weight as the decision about launching a new product. When everything is important, nothing is. The physical signals I described, the sweaty palms and elevated heart rate, are your early warning system that this isn't a normal decision. Use those signals to differentiate between everyday decisions and the ones that really matter.

- **Commitment Failure.** You know it's a big decision, but you optimize instead of decide. You gather more data, run more scenarios, seek more opinions, all to avoid the moment of choosing. You're not looking for information, though; you're looking for permission to do what you already know is right.

- **Narrative Failure.** You make the big decision but don't tell the story afterward. The decision happens in isolation instead of becoming part of your organization's mythology. Burke didn't just recall Tylenol; he went on *60 Minutes* to tell the world why. The story of the decision became more powerful than the decision itself. Don't miss the opportunity to leverage yours.

Awareness is your greatest leverage. Whether you blur the importance of decisions, hesitate when it counts, or overlook the story that gives your choices meaning, once you see your patterns, you can change them. Name your failure point, interrupt it, and choose again.

The Successor Question

Andy Grove and Gordon Moore, Intel's legendary leadership team, had a technique for breaking through decision paralysis that I now use religiously. They called it the Successor Question.

In 1985, Intel was hemorrhaging money in the memory chip business they'd founded the company on. But they couldn't bring themselves to exit. It was their identity, their history, their core. During one particularly brutal board meeting, Grove turned to Moore and asked, "If we got kicked out and the board brought in new management, what do you think they'd do?"

Moore answered immediately, "They'd get out of memory chips."

Grove stared at him for a moment, then inquired, "Why don't we walk out the door, come back in, and do it ourselves?"[44]

That question, "What would our successor do?" cuts through all the emotional attachment, sunk costs, and identity confusion that clouds decision moments. Your successor doesn't care about your history, your ego, or your emotional investments. They only care about what needs to be done.[45]

When I'm stuck on a decision, I ask myself, "If someone else took over my life tomorrow, what would they do?" The answer is usually obvious, and uncomfortable. That discomfort is the signal that it's the right decision.

The Post-Decision Valley

As we've discussed, decision-making can and will be a challenging act for all of us at one time or another, but there's more to the story. Nobody talks about what happens immediately after you make a big decision. There's this valley of doubt that opens up, usually about forty-eight hours later, where your brain starts manufacturing all the ways this could go wrong.

Kennedy faced it the morning after calling Mrs. King when Southern newspapers exploded in outrage. Burke faced it when Wall Street analysts declared Tylenol dead.

This valley is where most people reverse their decisions or hedge them into meaninglessness. You announce a bold new direction, then immediately add caveats, exceptions, and escape clauses. You water down the decision until it's no longer a decision at all.

The valley is normal. It's your brain's way of processing the magnitude of what you've done. But reversing the decision because of post-decision doubt is like turning back to slavery because freedom is scary. Once you've crossed the point of no return, the only way out is through.

Decision Moments Are Everywhere

The stories I've shared in this chapter feel like historic moments because we know how they turned out. But at the time, Kennedy, Burke, and Tubman were just people facing choices, feeling scared, and deciding anyway.

Your decision moments might not make history books, but they follow the same pattern. The physical activation, the three-second window, the choice between safety and identity, and the post-decision valley all unfold in the same way, whether you're choosing to recall a hundred million dollars of product or choosing to have a difficult conversation with your teenager.

What matters isn't the scale of the decision. It's recognizing when you're at a point of no return and having the courage to cross it as the person *you* want to be, not the person fear wants you to be.

The universe is conspiring in your favor, but it requires you to make decisions that align with who you are rather than what feels safe. Every decision moment is an opportunity to declare your identity, to choose between versions of yourself.

The question isn't whether you'll face these moments. You will. The question is whether you'll recognize them, prepare for them in your Third Space, and leverage them to become who you're meant to be.

Teddy Roosevelt was right: the best thing is the right thing, the next best is the wrong thing, and the worst is nothing. But what he didn't say is that in decision moments, the right thing and the scary thing are usually the same thing.

Your next decision moment is coming. When your palms start to sweat and your heart starts to race, remember: that's not fear. That's your body recognizing that you're standing at a point of no return.

The only question is who will you be when you cross it?

"I've learned that people will forget what you said, people will forget what you did, but people will never forget how you made them feel."

MAYA ANGELOU

CHAPTER 7

RECOGNITION MOMENTS: PEOPLE ARE WAITING TO BE SEEN

"Grant just handed in his notice," my head of sales told me through the telephone.

What? I thought. *That can't be.* I had just returned from a family vacation in Parker, Arizona. I wasn't mentally ready for bad news.

Grant was one of those employees who made everything around him work better. He operated in the space between sales and customer service and was the person who brought new clients into the fold, helped existing clients expand their services, and talked people off the ledge when they were thinking about leaving. He was the glue. The kind of person you don't fully appreciate until they're gone, which is exactly the problem.

My first response was to try to change Grant's mind, but the damage was already done. He had checked out. He was moving on to something new, something he hoped would be better.

What killed me was the reason. Grant didn't leave for more money or a bigger title or some exciting opportunity he couldn't refuse. He left because he felt underappreciated. He left because our recognition program, the one I had built and championed and written about in books, had failed to see him. Not because he wasn't doing great work. He was doing exceptional work. But the system we had designed couldn't recognize what exceptional looked like in his particular role.

Grant worked in the spaces between departments, which meant he'd often fallen through the cracks of our recognition structure. Managers recognized their direct reports. Teams celebrated their own wins. But Grant's contributions didn't fit neatly into any single box. He made other people successful in ways that were hard to measure and easy to overlook.

I should have seen it. I didn't.

That loss became a turning point. Not immediately. First, it became a wound. I replayed the conversations we had had before he left, wondering what I could have said differently. I examined our recognition systems, looking for the flaw I had missed. I talked to his former teammates, trying to understand how someone so valuable could feel so invisible.

The answer was uncomfortable. Our recognition program was designed from the top down. Managers recognized employees. Leaders set the tone. The assumption was that authority figures would naturally see and appreciate great work. But Grant's work happened in the white space of our org chart, and nobody with authority was positioned to see it clearly.

The good news came years later. Grant eventually reached out. By then, he was tired of the new job, which hadn't turned out to be what was promised, and tired of a boss who'd made our flaws look minor by comparison. He missed the environment we had created. He wanted to come back.

In his absence, we had rebuilt everything. The recognition program that had failed him was gone, replaced by something fundamentally different. I got to tell him about the changes, about what we had learned from losing him, about how his departure had forced us to question assumptions we should have years earlier.

Grant came back. And he became part of the team that would carry us through the most challenging period in our company's history.

What losing him reminded everyone at PeopleG2 was that recognition isn't optional. It's how people know they matter. And when people know they matter, they give you their very best. And they stick around to help you build what comes next.

The Mathematics of Feeling Seen

Psychologist John Gottman spent decades studying what makes relationships work. By observing couples and tracking their interactions, he discovered what he called the magic ratio. For a relationship to remain stable and healthy, Gottman found that partners need at least five positive interactions for every negative one. Not two to one. Not three to one. Five to one. Below that threshold, relationships start to deteriorate regardless of how committed the partners seem.[46]

The ratio held true even in relationships that looked solid from the outside. Couples who seemed happy but had dipped below the 5:1 threshold during conflict were significantly more likely to divorce in the years that followed. Based largely on this single metric, Gottman's research team could predict divorce with over 90-percent accuracy.

Researchers have since applied Gottman's ratio to workplace settings and found remarkably similar patterns. A 2004 study evaluated the effectiveness of sixty leadership teams and found that the highest-performing teams averaged a ratio of 5.6 positive comments to every negative one.[47] Medium performers averaged about 2:1. The lowest performers experienced nearly three negative comments for every positive one.

The implications are staggering. Recognition isn't something nice you do when you have time. It's a mathematical requirement for healthy relationships and high-performing teams. Most organizations are operating way below the threshold, then wondering why engagement scores are flat and turnover keeps climbing.

Think about the typical employee experience. That likely includes performance reviews that focus on areas for

Figure 7.1. The 5:1 ratio.

improvement, feedback sessions framed around what went wrong, and managers who believe that not criticizing is the same as complimenting. The math doesn't work. If your team experiences three pieces of corrective feedback for every acknowledgment, you're not running a high-performing organization. You're slowly destroying the relationships that hold it together.

Grant's experience was a perfect example. He received plenty of feedback about how to improve his handoffs or tighten his processes. What he didn't receive, at least not in proportion, was recognition for what he did extraordinarily well. The ratio was inverted. And like Gottman's couples heading toward divorce, the relationship deteriorated until departure felt like the only option.

I used to think that big recognition failures caused big damage and small ones didn't matter much. A missed promotion would hurt. A forgotten birthday card? Minor. Forgettable. Not worth worrying about.

I was wrong.

A 2024 study published in the *Proceedings of the National Academy of Sciences* tracked something almost comically minor: whether managers at a national retail chain delivered birthday gifts and cards to employees on time.[48]

That's it. Birthday cards. Delivered late or not at all.

The researchers found that even this tiny lapse, something most leaders would dismiss as inconsequential, measurably increased employee absences and reduced working hours. The effect wasn't dramatic per incident. But it was real, trackable, and when multiplied across an organization, expensive.

Think about what that means. Not a missed promotion. Not a failure to recognize a major achievement. A birthday card. Late.

The researchers attributed the effect to the emotional response of feeling overlooked. When someone doesn't get recognized in even a small way, they don't reason through it logically. They don't think, *Well, my manager is busy, and birthdays are minor, and I shouldn't take it personally*. They feel unseen. And feeling unseen changes behavior.

This is why the ratio matters so much. It's not just about the magnitude of recognition. It's about the accumulation. Every small moment of acknowledgment builds the relationship. Every small moment of invisibility erodes it. Most managers focus on the big recognitions: the awards ceremonies and promotions and public praise. They miss that birthday cards might matter just as much.

Grant didn't leave because of one missed recognition. He left because of a thousand small ones that accumulated into a conclusion: nobody here sees me.

The Counterintuitive Truth

After Grant left, I started questioning everything about how we approached recognition. The first assumption I challenged was the most fundamental one: that recognition should flow from the top down.

We grow up receiving praise from authority figures. Parents praise children. Teachers praise students. Coaches praise athletes. It seems natural that the pattern should continue into work. Managers praise employees. Leaders praise teams. The CEO sets the tone.

But what if that assumption is entirely wrong?

The breakthrough came almost by accident. We were running an experiment with one team, trying different approaches to see what would move their engagement scores. We explicitly told the team's manager to step back from recognition and let employees own it. Peers would recognize peers. The manager would facilitate but not direct.

Within weeks, something shifted. The recognition that emerged was more specific, more heartfelt, and more frequent than anything the manager had produced. People noticed things about their colleagues that managers couldn't see. They appreciated contributions that only someone working alongside them would understand.

When a peer takes time to acknowledge your contribution, it hits differently than when a manager does it. Peers have nothing to gain from recognizing you. They're not evaluating your performance or managing your development. They're not building a case for your next review or softening you up for a difficult assignment. Their recognition is a pure signal, uncorrupted by hierarchical dynamics.

We rolled the approach across the company. The shift took time. People were initially skeptical that leadership wasn't watching the numbers. They waited to see if we really meant it. When they realized we did, recognition transformed from a program into a practice.

After six months under the new system, employee engagement scores were up 25 percent. Customer service scores from clients had gone up 35 percent. Under the old system, people waited for authority figures to notice. If they didn't, employees felt deflated. In the new system, we were all part of the solution, and we built on a constant flow of positivity and appreciation that no manager could have created alone.

Grant would have thrived in this environment. The people working alongside him would have seen what I missed. They would have recognized his ability to navigate difficult client conversations, his patience with confused new customers, his talent for smoothing the friction between departments. Peer recognition would have caught what management recognition couldn't.

That's the counterintuitive truth: the most powerful recognition doesn't come from above. It comes from alongside.

Team All Blacks, Who Clean Their Own Toilets

The New Zealand All Blacks is arguably the most dominant team in the history of professional sports. Since their first international match in 1903, they have maintained a winning percentage of over 77 percent and have won three Rugby World Cup titles. In a sport played by nations across the globe, a small island country of fewer than five million people has built and sustained excellence for over a century.

What makes them so successful isn't just talent or coaching or tradition. It's culture. And at the heart of that culture is a ritual so counterintuitive it deserves examination: after every match, the senior players grab brooms and clean the locker room.[49]

They call it "sweeping the sheds."

I first heard this story from Richard Gilhooly, the general manager of people for New Zealand Rugby. We met after I gave a keynote in Johannesburg, and he spent hours teaching me how rugby actually works.

When we got to the "sweeping the sheds" part of the story, Richard told me that the origins trace back to a test match against England at Twickenham. After the All Blacks won, coach Steve Hansen looked around at the mess and said, "Geez, bloody pigsty this place, might as well clean it up." Then he started sweeping. The players joined in. When the custodial staff arrived, the players refused to let them take over.[50]

That moment became tradition. Now, regardless of whether the All Blacks have just won a World Cup final or lost a crucial match, the most senior players pick up brooms and sweep. Not the rookies. Not the support staff. The legends. The stars.

Former All Black Andrew Mehrtens explains it as personal discipline, not expecting someone else to do your job for you. Dan Carter, widely considered the greatest fly-half in rugby history, wrote about it in his book *The Art of Winning*. The strength of what they do, he explained, is that it's not the young player who sweeps the sheds. It's just the first person who grabs the broom, because no individual is bigger than the team.[51]

What does this have to do with recognition? Everything.

Recognition isn't just about applauding achievement. It's about demonstrating value through action. When a two-time World Rugby Player of the Year picks up a broom, he's recognizing every member of the support staff who cleans locker rooms for a living. He's recognizing that his success is built on the invisible contributions of hundreds of people who will never lift a trophy.

Sweeping the sheds is recognition expressed as humility. It says, "I see you." Your work matters. No task is beneath anyone who wears this jersey. That message echoes through the entire organization, creating a culture where everyone feels valued because the highest performers demonstrate that value daily.

This is what bottom-up recognition looks like at its purest. The stars recognizing the support staff. The celebrated acknowledging the invisible. Recognition flowing in every direction, not just downward from management to employees.

Eight Years of Handwritten Cards

For the last eight years I led PeopleG2, I wrote personal holiday cards to everyone connected to our company. Not just employees. Contractors. Key vendors. Anyone who had contributed to what we had built. The number grew each year as the company expanded. By the final year before I sold, the count was over 3,500 cards.

I started each October. My goal was to write roughly seventy cards per day, working Monday through Friday, to finish before Christmas. Some days I hit the target. Some days I fell short and had to catch up on weekends. By November, my hand would ache constantly and I would develop a callus on my middle finger from gripping the pen.

But the physical strain was nothing compared with the mental load. I never wanted an employee to compare cards with a colleague and realize I was writing on autopilot. Each card needed to be real. For employees I knew well, the words flowed naturally. Stories we shared, challenges we overcame together, specific moments that mattered. But for people I hadn't interacted with directly since their onboarding, I had to do research. I reached out to managers and teammates. I asked about specific projects, challenges overcome, qualities that made each person valuable.

Some cards were hard because I didn't know the person well enough. They had done their jobs without standing out, which is fine, but the cards would end up feeling generic when that happened. The struggle to find something specific to say taught me something about my own attention: if I couldn't write a meaningful card, it meant I hadn't been paying meaningful attention.

The point of all those hours wasn't to be thanked for my efforts. It was to close the loop. To ensure that everyone knew we appreciated them, that we knew how they had contributed and how their work had impacted the company. It was about them, not about me. Senior leaders would occasionally share stories they heard from their teams about what the cards meant, but I didn't need the feedback. The act itself was the point.

One email did stop me cold, though. A woman named Tamara from our client services department wrote to thank me, then added, "I didn't know you knew I existed."

I sat with those words for a long time.

Tamara had worked for us for four years. She was good at her job, got solid reviews from her manager, and was exactly the kind of quiet, consistent contributor who keeps companies running but rarely makes waves. For four years, we had green flag systems and team celebrations and all the right recognition programs. None of it had convinced her that the CEO knew her name.

One handwritten card did what four years of systems could not.

Those cards took me hundreds of hours. They were probably the best investment of time I made in my twenty years as CEO.

Recognizing the Journey

Recognition doesn't only happen at work.

A few weeks after my wife's final surgery, we were sitting in a doctor's office at Cedars-Sinai in Los Angeles. The surgeon was reviewing my wife's latest test results, confirming what we had been hoping and praying for. No cerebrospinal fluid leak outside her brain. The stuff that had caused all the headaches and pain? It was gone. The surgery had worked. The nightmare was ending.

As the doctor left the room, my wife turned to me and thanked me for helping her through that horrible period of her life.

"I would not be alive today without these doctors. Or without you," she affirmed.

After years of advocating for her in hospital rooms, fighting with insurance companies, questioning diagnoses that didn't feel right, holding her hand through procedures that terrified us both, she recognized what I had done.

That moment of recognition meant more than any professional acknowledgment I've ever received. Not just because it came from someone important, but because it came from someone who knew exactly what it had cost. My wife had witnessed every sleepless night, every difficult conversation with medical staff, every moment when I wanted to give up but didn't. Her recognition was specific because she had been there for all of it.

This is what makes recognition powerful. Not the words themselves but the weight of understanding behind the words. When someone who truly knows what you've done recognizes you, it lands differently than generic praise from someone who only saw the outcome.

The Three Catalysts That Multiply Impact

Not all recognition is created equal. Some moments land and some moments evaporate. After watching thousands of recognition exchanges over two decades, I've identified three factors that separate forgettable acknowledgments from moments that change how people see themselves.

The first is specificity. Generic praise is barely better than no praise at all. "Great job!" communicates that you noticed something but couldn't be bothered to identify what. Specific recognition names the action, explains the impact, and connects to the larger purpose. It requires observation, which requires presence. You cannot give specific recognition if you haven't been paying attention.

The second catalyst is witnesses. Private recognition matters, but public recognition multiplies. When someone is acknowledged in front of peers, the moment becomes shared memory. Other people see what gets valued. The recognition becomes a teaching moment for the entire organization, not just a private transaction between two people.

The third catalyst is surprise. Expected recognition loses power through predictability. "Employee of the Month" programs fail partly because everyone knows exactly when the moment is coming. The monthly rhythm becomes background noise. Surprise recognition lands harder because it emerges organically from genuine appreciation rather than calendared obligation.

When specificity, witnesses, and surprise combine, recognition moments become exponentially more powerful.

Reading the Room Before They Ask

In chapter 3, I introduced the concept of High Sensory Tuning, the practice of regulating your own nervous system so you can accurately read what's happening in a given moment. That includes reading into how other people are feeling, and nowhere is this skill more essential than in recognition.

Most leaders wait for achievement to trigger recognition. Someone hits a goal, closes a deal, completes a project, and then gets acknowledged for the visible result. This approach entirely misses the most important recognition opportunities.

People need recognition before they ask for it. They need it when they're struggling, not just when they're succeeding. They need it when they're quietly grinding through difficult work that won't produce measurable outcomes for months.

The tragedy is that by the time someone asks for recognition, they've often been suffering the absence of it for a long time. Grant never asked. He just left. Tamara never demanded acknowledgment. She simply concluded, after four years, that leadership didn't know she existed.

High Sensory Tuning means reading the early signals. It means paying special attention to the person who's been unusually quiet in meetings. Or the team member whose enthusiasm seems dimmed. Or the contributor who used to share ideas freely but has retreated into just completing assigned tasks. These are recognition deficits in formation. Left unaddressed, they become disengagement, then departure.

Before entering any meeting or interaction, pause and ask yourself who in the room might need recognition that they're unlikely to seek. Then look for an opportunity to provide it. Not forced or awkward, but genuine. Something you actually noticed and appreciated, delivered at a moment when they didn't expect it.

The Diagnostic Framework

Like all the moments described in this section, recognition moments have predictable failure patterns.

If you struggle to identify who needs recognition, you're probably only seeing the loud contributors. The squeaky wheels get the acknowledgment while the quiet performers remain invisible. You're waiting for achievement rather than looking for effort. The solution is systematic observation: who on your team is contributing in ways that don't naturally attract attention?

If you struggle to show up in recognition moments, you're probably defaulting to generic praise because you haven't done the observation work required for specificity. "Great job!" is what you say when you weren't paying close enough attention to say what was actually great. The solution is presence: get close enough to your team's work that you can name specific behaviors that mattered.

If you struggle to leverage recognition after the moment, you're keeping acknowledgment private when it should be public. You're not telling the stories that turn individual recognition into a cultural signal. The solution is propagation: make recognition visible, shareable, and story-worthy.

Here are three methods you can apply in your personal or professional life to create better recognition moments:

1. **The Specificity Formula**

    When recognizing someone, use this structure: "I noticed when you [specific action] and it [specific impact] because [connection to larger purpose]."

    Example: "I noticed when you completely restructured the client proposal after that difficult feedback meeting. The client specifically mentioned how the revision addressed their concerns, and that saved a relationship we've been building for three years."

2. **The Third Space for Recognition**

    Before any interaction where recognition might be appropriate, take thirty seconds to prepare.

    First, regulate your own state so you can read others accurately. Second, identify who might need recognition. Third, recall specific observations you can draw on. Fourth, enter the interaction ready to see people, not just manage tasks.

3. **Future-Casting Your Recognition**

    Once a week, look ahead at your calendar and team situation. Ask yourself, "Who will face a challenging moment in the coming days? Who has been quietly contributing without recent acknowledgment? What specific observations can I make this week that will fuel recognition later? Where can I position myself to witness moments worth recognizing?"

The Echo Chamber You Want

Maya Angelou's observation that people never forget how you made them feel is not just wisdom. It's neuroscience.[52] Our brains encode emotional experiences more deeply than factual ones. The feeling of being recognized, truly seen and valued, creates memory traces that persist long after the specific words fade.

This is why recognition moments have a disproportionate impact. They don't just make people feel good temporarily. They shape how people understand their own value and their relationship to an organization. A single powerful recognition moment can overwrite months of feeling invisible.

Recognition creates an echo chamber, but unlike the negative connotation that phrase usually carries, this is an echo chamber you want. When recognition flows freely, it bounces back. People who feel recognized become recognizers themselves. The culture amplifies appreciation rather than dampening it.

Tamara's story has a coda. After receiving my card, she started giving more green flags to her teammates. She told her manager that the experience of feeling seen had made her realize how important it was to help others feel seen. One moment of recognition cascaded into dozens more.

Grant's story has a better ending than it deserved. He came back, and he brought with him a new appreciation for what we had built, something he couldn't see until he'd experienced its absence. During COVID, Grant was part of the team that developed three breakthrough ideas for how we would not just survive but thrive, including steps that would lead us to become the first company to provide COVID tests directly to consumers. Grant was a big part of that win.

Sometimes the people who leave teach you what you needed to learn. Sometimes they come back and help you build something better. Either way, their departure becomes a gift if you're willing to receive it.

Your people are waiting to be seen. Some of them, like Tamara, have been waiting for years. Some of them, like Grant, won't wait much longer. They won't ask for it. They'll simply conclude, eventually, that no one knows they exist. And then they'll leave.

Unless you see them first.

For the Recognition Ratio Calculator and peer recognition program templates, visit chrisdyer.com/moments.

"We are like islands in the sea, separate on the surface but connected in the deep."

WILLIAM JAMES

CHAPTER 8

CONNECTION MOMENTS: THE INVISIBLE EQUITY

During my wife's medical crises, I learned something about connection that changed how I understand the word entirely.

When people heard what we were going through, the strokes, the surgeries, the months of uncertainty, they said something that I'm sure you've said too. I've said it myself dozens of times, believing I was being supportive.

"Let me know if you need anything."

Those might be the seven most useless words in the English language.

I don't say that to be harsh. The intention behind them is genuine. People mean it when they say it. But here's what happens when you're drowning: you don't have the capacity to identify what you need, formulate a request, and reach out to the person who offered. You're using every ounce of energy just to survive the next hour. The cognitive load of converting a vague offer into a specific ask is more than you can bear.

So you say, "Thanks, I will," but you never do. Meanwhile, the person who offered feels like they did something, when what they actually did was transfer the burden of connection back to the person least equipped to carry it.

Then there were the others.

My best friend, Mark, showed up at my house with his toolbox while I was at the hospital. He didn't ask what needed fixing. He walked through the house, tightened the loose cabinet hinges, replaced the smoke detector batteries, fixed the running toilet that had been annoying us for months. When I got home, these small broken things that had been silently adding to my stress were just handled. He never asked permission. He just showed up with his toolbox and did it.

Another friend made us dinner every Friday night for months. Not once did she ask, "Would you like me to bring food?" She simply texted, "Leaving chicken piccata on the porch at 6," and it appeared. Every Friday. For months. She gave us one less decision to make. One less thing to manage. One moment each week when I didn't have to figure out how to feed my family.

My senior staff stopped asking if I needed help with work. They just covered meetings, handled clients, made decisions that would normally require my input. They didn't wait for permission or instructions. They saw the gap and filled it. When I had capacity again, they briefed me on what I'd missed. Not once did they make me feel like I owed them something for doing it. They simply showed up.

Even my neighbor, someone I'd waved to but barely knew, started picking up our mail whenever I asked. But here's the thing: I only had to ask once. After that, he just did it. He saw the mail piling up, grabbed it, and left it inside our screen door. No fanfare. No need for thanks. Just a quiet, consistent presence.

This is what connection actually looks like. Not offering. Doing. Not asking what someone needs. Seeing what they need and providing it. Not waiting for an invitation. Showing up with your toolbox.

The people who said, "Let me know if you need anything," were being kind. The people who showed up with chicken piccata were creating connection. Both cared about us. Only one group's care actually landed.

What Makes a Connection Moment

A nice interaction is pleasant and forgettable. You have dozens of them every week. They don't change anything.

A connection moment changes the relationship. Both people share something true. Both feel unmistakably heard. Both leave with something specific: a next step, a shift in understanding, a bond that didn't exist before.

The friends with the toolbox and the Friday dinners weren't just being helpful. They were communicating something profound: I see you. I see what you're going through. You don't have to carry this alone, and you don't have to manage me while you're drowning. I'm just going to be here, doing what needs to be done.

That's connection. Not the offer. The action. Not the words. The presence.

Lincoln's Gift for Connection

Abraham Lincoln understood something about connection that most leaders miss entirely.[53]

During the Civil War, Lincoln spent hours walking through camps, talking with individual soldiers about their families and fears. He remembered names and details from previous conversations. His generals found this baffling. There was a war to win. Why was the president talking to privates about their farms back in Ohio?

Lincoln knew something they didn't: wars are won by people who believe their leader sees them as people, not as resources to be deployed.

His relationship with Ulysses Grant exemplified this further. Previous commanders required constant management. When Lincoln found Grant, he did something extraordinary: he trusted him. Lincoln saw Grant clearly, understood his strengths and weaknesses, and chose to believe in him.

"I can't spare this man," Lincoln reportedly spoke of Grant. "He fights."

Grant gave Lincoln something rare: honesty without political calculation. After Lincoln was assassinated, Grant wept openly. The connection had transcended strategy.

This is what connection does in organizations, in families, in any human system. It creates bonds that survive difficulty. It transforms transactions into relationships. It turns followers into believers.

The Barrier Isn't Skill

Researcher Nicholas Epley at the University of Chicago Booth School of Business conducted an experiment that revealed something counterintuitive about connection.[54]

He randomly assigned commuters on Chicago trains to one of three conditions: start a conversation with the stranger next to them, sit in solitude, or commute as they normally would. Before the experiment, participants in all groups predicted that talking to strangers would be the least pleasant option. They expected awkwardness, rejection, discomfort.

The results told a different story. Commuters assigned to talk to strangers reported significantly higher well-being than those assigned to sit in silence. The conversations weren't awkward. They were energizing. People enjoyed connecting far more than they had predicted.

This is why regular commuters don't strike up conversations on their own. We systematically underestimate how much both we and others want to connect. Epley calls this a "psychological barrier" to connection. The barrier isn't skill. Most people are perfectly capable of having a meaningful conversation. The barrier is permission. We've convinced ourselves that others don't want to be bothered, that reaching out is intrusive, that connection attempts will be unwelcome.

We're wrong. Almost always, we're wrong.

The person you've been meaning to call but haven't? They want to hear from you. The colleague you've been wanting to know better? They'd welcome the conversation. The neighbor you wave to but have never really talked with? They're waiting for someone to break through the polite distance.

Connection isn't a talent that some people have and others don't. It's a choice that fear prevents us from making. The seven useless words in "let me know if you need anything" are often spoken because we're afraid to presume, afraid to impose, afraid to show up uninvited with our toolbox.

But the people drowning in crisis don't need us to protect our own comfort. They need us to show up.

Facts Versus Genuine Knowing

Dr. Peterson, my childhood pediatrician, would consult a small notecard before each visit. On it, he'd scribbled facts about my hobbies and activities. "So Chris," he'd inquire, glancing at the card, "how's soccer going?"

Except I had quit soccer. I was on the swim team now. Had been for over a year.

His intentions were good. He was trying to build rapport, to make a kid feel seen and valued, but the execution missed the mark entirely. Instead of feeling known, I felt processed. The notecard system, meant to create connection, actually highlighted how little connection existed. He had facts about me without actually knowing me.

This became a formative lesson that shaped how I thought about connection at PeopleG2. At our peak, we had over 3,500 employees and independent contractors, spread across the country. I couldn't possibly know every detail about every person. But I could create systems and expectations that ensured that leaders throughout the organization actually knew their people.

I expected every leader to know key information about the fifty or so people they worked with most closely. Their spouse or partner's names. Their kids' names. Family situations. Personal dreams and challenges. Not because we would quiz them but because this knowledge fundamentally changes how you lead.

But here's what I learned from Dr. Peterson's notecard: knowing facts is not the same as connection. The facts have to be deployed with genuine curiosity, in the right moments, with real presence. Robotically mentioning someone's spouse once a month on a random call doesn't create connection. It creates the feeling of being managed.

The friend who showed up with his toolbox didn't consult a notecard. He knew me well enough to know that small broken things were adding to my stress. He knew that I wouldn't ask for help. He knew that doing was more valuable than offering. That's not information. That's connection.

Someone Who Saw Me

My grandfather, Papa Jack, and Uncle Lee, whom you met in chapter 2, were brothers. They were also two men who shaped how I understand moments. Uncle Lee taught me about seeing the true moment hiding inside the obvious one. Papa Jack taught me something different: how connection can be an act of radical belief.

When I turned fifteen and got my learner's permit, Papa Jack offered to come over and let me practice driving with him. This was typical of him. He was always offering help, always finding ways to spend time together, always present in my life in ways that felt natural rather than obligatory.

He arrived at the house, and we got in the car together. I was nervous, the way any fifteen-year-old is when they're still learning to control a two-ton machine. I turned on the ignition, carefully checked my mirrors, backed out of the driveway, and started down the street.

That's when Papa Jack tilted his seat back and decided to take a nap.

I looked over at him, confused. "What are you doing?"

"I know you got this," he assured me. "I might as well take a nap."

Can you imagine giving someone that much confidence? Demonstrating your belief in them by falling asleep, not worrying one bit that they might crash the car or make some other perilous mistake? He was there if I needed him. He was there if I had a problem. But he trusted me so completely that he saw no reason to stay awake and micromanage.

I drove for hours that day. All around the neighborhood, practicing my parallel parking, navigating intersections, building the skills I would need for my driving test. And the whole time, Papa Jack was snoring away in the passenger seat, giving me probably the greatest gift of confidence I've ever received.

That's connection through belief. He saw me as capable before I saw myself that way. His certainty became my certainty.

The Woman Who Saved Us

Before my wife and I adopted our children, my mother-in-law moved in with us. She had just gone through a divorce and needed a place to land. We agreed to share a quiet home together, three adults finding their rhythm.

Then we brought home three kids from Russia over the span of eleven months, and quiet became chaos.

My mother-in-law could have left. She could have said this wasn't what she signed up for, that she needed peace after her divorce, that raising someone else's children wasn't her responsibility. Instead, she became "Babushka."

During my wife's medical crises, when I was at the hospital or working or just trying to hold myself together, Babushka held everything else. I would come home after midnight from sitting with my wife at the hospital and find her folding laundry, the house somehow still functioning. Dinner would be ready when I walked in, even though I hadn't asked, even though I wouldn't have thought to ask. The kids didn't even notice we were gone because Babushka had it handled.

The sheer volume of what she did, the cooking, the cleaning, the parenting, the emotional labor of making three traumatized children feel safe while their mother was fighting for her life, I could never properly articulate. She didn't offer to help. She didn't ask what we needed. She just became the infrastructure that kept our family from collapsing.

She has passed now. But we remember her often, especially when we talk about what saved us during those years. Not the doctors, though they were essential. Not the treatments, though they worked. What saved us was the people who showed up without being asked. And no one showed up more completely than Babushka.

This is what it feels like to receive connection during crisis. Not words. Presence. Not offers. Action. Not, "Let me know if you need anything." Folded laundry at midnight and dinner on the table and children who didn't notice that their world was falling apart.

Saving Something Precious

The year before COVID hit, my book club read *The Art of Gathering* by Priya Parker.[55] As we discussed the book, my friend Cecilia mentioned that her parents belonged to a music club that had existed for three and a half decades. Every month, they gathered to share music with each other.

I was fascinated. How does a group sustain itself for that long? I begged Cecilia to get me an invitation. It took almost a year. Finally, when it was her parents' turn to host, Cecilia was able to bring me along as a guest.

The twelve members were mostly in their late seventies and eighties, with some in their nineties. I was in my mid-forties, decades younger than anyone else in the room. The format was elegant: each person would play a song, no more than ten minutes, that fit the evening's theme. After the listening portion of the evening, they shared a meal and conversation.

Much to my surprise, they invited me back the next month. And this time, they said, bring your lovely bride.

My wife was skeptical. The theme that month was "Play music that represents an instrument you wish you would have learned as a child." The other members chose pieces by Chopin,

Bach, Beethoven. My wife played Def Leppard because she wished she would have learned the drums.

I think she was hoping to be kicked out. Instead, the group loved it. They asked us to join permanently.

Then COVID hit.

Suddenly, I was on the email chain as the group discussed what seemed inevitable. Music Club was over. This incredible run of thirty-five years was going to end. They couldn't meet in person. It was too dangerous.

That's when I stepped in. "Do you know we can do this on Zoom?"

I got back ten or twelve responses: "What is a Zoom?"

So I taught them. One by one, I walked members through how to download the software, how to join a meeting, how to share their screen. We figured out together how to preserve what they'd built.

It saved Music Club. The technology I knew became the bridge that kept them connected.

As of the writing of this book, my wife and I are still in Music Club. Some members have passed away, and we've dedicated entire sessions to their memory, playing music they would have chosen. What strikes me most is what they've taught me about death and acceptance. These members, thirty and forty years my senior, have a level-headed approach to mortality that I hope I can develop someday.

They have taught me that connection can survive loss. That community is resilient if you invest in it. That the gift of belonging to something larger than yourself is worth fighting for.

When Connection Fails Despite Everything

I need to share something I've protected for years.

My son Dmitri is one of the three children my wife and I adopted from Russia in 2006. In chapter 3, I told the story of the plane nearly crashing on our way to bring home our daughter Luba, the terror of losing three engines over the

Pacific. What I haven't told publicly is what happened afterward with Dmitri.

My son suffers from drug addiction and mental illness. During his teenage years, we tried everything we could think of to help him through it. Every program imaginable. Every intervention. Every treatment center. Every approach that desperate parents reach for when they're watching their child slip away. Then, when he turned eighteen, he decided he'd had enough. He wanted to live on the streets.

Since that day, he has spent as much time homeless as he has homed. He comes in and out of our lives in pockets. Sometimes he's accepting help, wanting to get better, showing up as the son I always hoped he'd become. Sometimes he's diving deeper down, closer to death than I can bear to think about.

There came a point when I had to mourn something I never expected to grieve: the relationship I thought we would have. The wedding I hoped to attend. The grandchildren I wanted to have. The career he could build. The conversations we could have over holiday dinners.

Every time my phone rings from a number I don't recognize, my chest tightens. The call could be Dmitri with a new phone number. It could be a call from jail. Or from a hospital. Or it could be that final call, the one where someone tells me the drugs won.

As I write this book, Dmitri has checked into another program. He's trying to maintain sobriety, to avoid going back to jail. I hope it works this time. I've hoped before.

I share this not for sympathy but because this chapter is about connection, and I cannot write honestly about connection without acknowledging that some connections break despite everything we do to maintain them. My family and I showed up for Dmitri with everything we had. Toolboxes and Friday dinners and years of presence. Sometimes the person you're trying to connect with isn't able to receive it. That's not a failure of your practice. It's a reality of human relationships.

Connection is not a guaranteed outcome. It's an ongoing practice. And sometimes, despite our best efforts, the practice fails.

But that doesn't mean we stop practicing.

Connections That Take Years

Not every connection pays off immediately. Some take years. Some never produce any measurable return.

I met Ali Payani years ago through work. He handled some of our marketing needs, and from the beginning, I felt that sense you sometimes get with certain people: we were destined to do something meaningful together. The timing just wasn't right.

We stayed connected. We helped each other when we could. We maintained the relationship even when there was no immediate transaction to justify it. Years passed. Then the right opportunity emerged, and we launched EngageBeast.ai together.

The invisible equity compounds. Every genuine connection you make adds to a reservoir of trust that you can draw on when times get hard. You can't manufacture this equity overnight. You build it slowly, through thousands of small moments when you choose presence over efficiency, doing over offering, showing up over standing by.

The Third Space for Connection

As it does with recognition, the Third Space takes a particular form when applied to connection. We often assume that connecting with other people is automatic, that because we're in the same room or on the same call, we're truly *with* them. But being present with another human being is work. It requires emotional availability, cognitive bandwidth, and a willingness to set aside whatever came before. Unless you deliberately prepare yourself for that work, you end up carrying your last meeting, your last conflict, or your last worry straight into the next interaction.

Before any interaction where connection is possible, you need to reset. Not just physically move from one meeting to the next but actually prepare your nervous system to be present with another human being.

The Third Space for connection means taking thirty seconds before an important conversation to ask yourself, "Am I actually ready to be here? Have I set down the last thing so I can pick up this thing? Am I prepared to give this person my full attention?"

The energy shift when real connection happens is palpable. You can feel the moment when someone moves from guarded to open, from performing to authentic, from transactional to relational. But you can only sense that shift if you've done the Third Space work to be present enough to notice it.

The Diagnostic Framework

As with the types of moments we've previously discussed, connection moments have predictable failure patterns. Here are three you might be experiencing right now:

- **Identification Failure.** You're waiting for "big" moments and missing daily ones. They might be as small and seemingly inconsequential as the thirty-second conversation before a meeting or during the walk to the parking lot, but they matter.

- **Commitment Failure.** You're multitasking when you should be focusing on potential connections, present but not present. Put down the phone. Turn your body to face the person you're interacting with. You'll be amazed at how fully you'll show up once your mind isn't somewhere else.

- **Narrative Failure.** You're treating connections as one-time events, but continuity creates meaningful narratives. When someone shares something meaningful, check in on it later. If they mention they're percolating their next big idea or dreading their ex's upcoming wedding or planning a thirtieth birthday party for a geriatric cat, remember it and return to it later. Those small callbacks show that you were listening, that you cared enough to hold onto the details, and that the person matters to you beyond the moment. Connection happens in that quiet continuity of attention.

The Connection Moment Tool Kit

If you've been struggling to make or sustain connections, or if you want to deepen the connections you already have, try these strategies:

- **Stop Offering; Start Doing.** The next time someone is struggling, don't say, "Let me know if you need anything." Identify one specific thing and do it. Bring food. Mow their lawn. Don't ask permission. Just show up with your toolbox.

- **The Three Catalysts.** Connection accelerates through vulnerability (sharing something real), specificity (noticing something particular about the person you're connecting with), and follow-through (remembering what they shared and asking about it later). All three require presence. All three require doing, not just offering. If connections aren't happening the way you expect, spend time identifying which of these three components you're skipping out on and take steps to improve each one. This may involve sharing more of yourself, being more observant, or taking greater care to maintain connective threads.

- **The Seven-Minute Investment.** Once a day, give one person seven minutes of your complete, undivided attention. Not while checking email. Not while thinking about what you'll say next. Seven minutes when your only job is to understand them.

- **Future-Casting Your Connections.** Once a week, look ahead and ask yourself, "Who in my life will face a challenging moment in the coming days? Who might need connection that they won't ask for?" Then don't offer. Do.

The Connection We Cannot Force

I opened this chapter with the people who showed up during my wife's crises because that's what connection looks like when it works. But I included Dmitri because connection is not something we can guarantee.

We can do everything right. We can show up with presence and action and years of consistency. We can love fiercely and unconditionally. Yet sometimes, the connection we long for doesn't happen.

That doesn't mean we stop practicing. It means we accept that connection is a practice, not an outcome. We keep extending our hand even when it isn't taken. We keep the door open even when the person we love chooses to stay outside.

With Dmitri, I keep practicing. I keep making myself available. I keep loving him in whatever way he can receive it. And I've made peace with the reality that the outcome isn't in my control. The only thing I control is whether I keep showing up.

That's the hardest lesson about connection: it requires two people, and you can only be responsible for one of them.

Figure 8.1. Separate on the surface, connected in the deep.

But it's also the most liberating. Because when you release attachment to outcomes and focus only on your own showing up, connection becomes simpler. Not easier but simpler. You do your part. You do it fully. And you trust that what's supposed to happen will happen.

The invisible equity you build through connection doesn't guarantee anything. But it makes everything more possible.

"We are like islands in the sea," William James wrote. Separate on the surface but connected in the deep.

Your job is to dive. Not to offer to dive if someone needs you. To actually dive.

"The truth will set you free, but first it will piss you off."

GLORIA STEINEM

CHAPTER 9

TRUTH MOMENTS: THE PROFITABLE PAIN

In 2009, I joined a CEO peer group called ABL. The Adaptive Business Leaders roundtable met monthly, and part of the process was that each CEO would take a turn presenting their business to the group for feedback. These sessions could be brutal. The gloves came off. Everyone said what needed to be said to help that CEO improve their business, regardless of how uncomfortable it might be to hear.

After a few months, my turn came. I walked the group through PeopleG2, our challenges with the recession, our strategy for survival. I thought I was prepared for tough questions. I was not prepared for James Meyers.

James looked at me across the table and said something that felt like a punch to the chest: "Maybe you're not the right person to be CEO."

I sat there, stunned. He repeated his thought.

"You might not be the best person to be the CEO of your own company."

Talk about hard truth.

His words repeated in my head for months. In the shower. Driving to work. Lying awake at 2 AM. *Maybe you're not the right person. Maybe you're not the best person.* The idea would surface at random moments, always with that same gut-punch feeling.

Then, somewhere around month three, something shifted. I realized James was right. In a way. He didn't mean I should resign and hand the keys to someone else. He meant I needed to evolve. I needed to become a better CEO. The person I was in that moment wasn't equipped to lead the company through what was coming. I had to transform.

And that's exactly what I did.

Hard truths are often impossible to swallow whole. Your immediate reaction to hearing a truth like that is almost guaranteed to differ from your final reaction. James delivered the truth to me in February. I didn't fully receive it until May. That gap, those months of processing and resistance and eventual acceptance, is where transformation happens. Most of us give up on truth too quickly, assuming our initial reaction is the verdict. It's not. It's just the beginning.

The Employee Who Quit and Came Back

As uncomfortable as hard truths are to receive, they can also be uncomfortable to deliver. When it was my turn to be the dreaded bearer, years after James delivered his truth to me, I started to appreciate his courage.

Carrie, a woman on our sales team, had tremendous potential. She was smart and personable and clients loved her. But she was allowing her personal life to bleed so far into her workday that she never achieved her goals. The chaos at home followed her to her desk, into her calls, through her entire week. Month after month, she fell short of targets that should have been easy for someone with her abilities.

During a transition in our sales leadership, I stepped in to lead the team temporarily. That's when I really saw what was happening. Carrie would spend the first couple of hours or so of each workday dealing with personal crises. Calls from family members, financial emergencies, relationship drama. By the time she started actual work, half the morning was gone. The pattern repeated after lunch. By end of day, she'd have put in maybe four productive hours while her colleagues did eight.

Something had to be done. I called her into my office and said the quiet part out loud.

I told her what I was observing. I explained that her personal chaos was bleeding into her professional life and preventing her from becoming the salesperson she was capable of being. I said it with genuine care for her success. I wasn't trying to hurt her. I was trying to help her see something she couldn't see herself.

She got upset. She cried. And then she quit.

We were genuinely sorry to see her go. We liked her. She had amazing potential. But the chaos of her life was impacting everything, and she wasn't ready to hear that truth.

Eighteen months later, my phone rang. It was Carrie.

She thanked me for what I had said. She apologized for how she'd reacted. She admitted it had taken her some time to process the truth, to figure out how to change, to get her life into better balance. What I'd told her had been painful to hear, but it had also been accurate. Once she could accept that, she could finally do something about it.

As it happened, we had an opening on the sales team. I asked if she wanted to give it another try.

This time, her tears were those of joy.

She came back and became an amazing employee for several years. But the part that still moves me is what happened next. She eventually became someone who would coach other employees who were struggling the way she once had. The truth that had made her cry and quit transformed her into a truth-teller herself. She could sit with struggling team members and say, "I know this is hard to hear, but I've been where you are, and this feedback might be exactly what you need."

The cycle completed. Truth received, processed, transformed into truth given.

The MUM Effect: Why We Stay Silent

Carrie and I may have made it look a little too easy. In reality, no one savors delivering tough news, and few of us are naturally good at it. Many of us will do just about anything to avoid it.

Our tendency to avoid delivering bad news is so ubiquitous, in fact, that researchers have a name for it: the MUM effect. It stands for "keeping mum about undesirable messages," and it's one of the most robust findings in organizational psychology.

Sidney Rosen and Abraham Tesser first documented the phenomenon in the 1970s.[56] They found that people will go to extraordinary lengths to avoid being the bearer of bad news, even when that avoidance causes significant harm. In one study, participants who had to deliver negative feedback about someone's test performance chose to distort the message, softening it until it was almost unrecognizable. Others simply refused to deliver the message at all, even when explicitly told that their silence would hurt the recipient.

The MUM effect isn't about being nice. It's about self-protection. We instinctively understand that delivering bad news associates us with that news. The messenger really does get shot, at least emotionally. So we stay silent. We soften. We hope someone else will say the hard thing so we don't have to.

Harvard professor Amy Edmondson's research on psychological safety reveals the organizational cost of this silence.[57] Teams in which people feel safe to speak uncomfortable truths dramatically outperform teams whose people stay mum. Her studies of hospital units found that the teams with the highest reported error rates weren't actually making more mistakes. They were the teams with enough psychological safety to admit mistakes openly. The "safe" teams, the ones with low reported errors, were actually making just as many mistakes but hiding them. And people were dying because of it.

Environments in which truth flows freely look worse on paper but perform better in reality. The mess of honest feedback is more productive than the tidiness of polite silence.

This maps directly to what I experienced at ABL. Those peer group sessions felt brutal. Everyone was saying hard things, after all. Our conflict was visible on the surface. But the companies led by CEOs in that room outperformed their peers precisely because we had created a container from which truth could flow. The MUM effect was suspended. We gave each other permission to say what needed to be said.

Radical Candor and the Care/ Directness Matrix

Not every truth, however, leads to positive metamorphosis, no matter how long you spend digesting it. Kim Scott, who led teams at Google and Apple before becoming a leadership coach, developed a framework that explains why some truths transform while others destroy.[58] She calls it Radical Candor, and it's built on two axes: how much you care personally about the person and how directly you're willing to challenge them.

When you challenge directly but don't show that you care, you get what Scott calls Obnoxious Aggression. This is the boss who delivers brutal feedback without any warmth. The truth might be accurate, but it lands as an attack. People become defensive, resentful, closed.

When you care personally but won't challenge directly, you get Ruinous Empathy. This is the manager who likes their team so much that they can't bring themselves to give honest feedback. They soften every criticism until it's meaningless. They tell themselves they're being kind, but they're actually being cruel by withholding the truth someone needs in order to grow because delivering it would be uncomfortable.

When you neither care nor challenge, you get Manipulative Insincerity. This is the political operator who says whatever serves their immediate interests. No truth, no care. Just moves on a chessboard.

The goal is caring personally while challenging directly. That's Radical Candor. When James Meyers told me I might not be the right CEO, he was demonstrating Radical Candor. He didn't say it to hurt me or to feel superior. He said it because he cared about my success and believed I could handle the truth. His directness was an act of respect.

When I delivered hard feedback to Carrie, I also wanted to do so with Radical Candor. The care had to come first, both in my preparation and in my delivery. Without it, the truth would have been just another attack from a boss who didn't understand her life.

Sheila Heen and Douglas Stone at the Harvard Negotiation Project have spent decades studying why some difficult conversations succeed while others fail.[59] Their research revealed that the problem usually isn't the delivery. It's the receiving.

Most advice about giving feedback focuses on the sender. Soften your tone. Use "I" statements. Sandwich criticism between compliments. But Heen and Stone found that even perfectly delivered feedback often fails because the recipient isn't equipped to receive it. They're triggered by the content, by who's delivering it, or by what it implies about their identity.

This explains why James's feedback took three months to land for me. His delivery was fine. The problem was my receiving. I wasn't ready to hear it. My identity as a successful founder was threatened. My ego was activated. I had to work through all of that before the truth could actually get through.

The implication for truth-tellers is that you can't control how your truth lands. You can prepare well, deliver with care, and still have it rejected. The only thing you can do is create conditions where receiving becomes more possible and then release attachment to the outcome.

The Truth I Didn't Tell

I need to tell you about a truth I didn't tell, and what it cost.

I've always had a strong gut feeling about people. I can usually read someone within minutes of meeting them and form an assessment that proves accurate over time. This instinct was honed in my first job out of college, working at a hotel where I eventually conducted hundreds of interviews. Once the general manager noticed I consistently hired great people, I became the person in charge of interviewing everyone. We were a new hotel and needed a full staff, so I got very good at reading candidates very quickly.

Professionally, I used this skill constantly. But in my personal relationships, I held back. I was afraid to upset friends or overstep boundaries. I watched many of them date people I knew were wrong for them. Real losers, frankly. And I said nothing.

My friend Becky was dating a guy I couldn't stand. From the first moment I met him, I had the worst feeling. Everything in my gut said this man was trouble. But I didn't say a word. It wasn't my place. What if I was wrong? What if she got angry with me? What if it damaged our friendship?

They got married. Within a year, they were divorced.

During that year, he was physically and mentally abusive. He took her money. He ran up debt in her name. He damaged her in ways that took years to heal.

After it was over, I apologized to Becky for not speaking up. She admitted that it might not have mattered. She might have married him anyway, convinced that love would conquer my concerns. We'll never know.

But she told me something that changed how I approach truth in relationships: she never got serious with anyone again without having me meet them first. She wanted access to my assessment. She wanted the truth I'd been too afraid to give her before.

The avoided truth didn't protect our friendship. It didn't protect her from a bad decision. It just guaranteed she'd make that decision without all the information she deserved to have. The cost of my silence was a year of abuse, financial ruin, and trauma that still affects her today.

Withheld truth is not kindness. It's cowardice dressed up as politeness. On the flipside, choosing truth means choosing someone else's well-being over your own comfort. At first, it may sting. For both of you. But if you've worked to develop meaningful connections, that truth is unlikely to break your relationship. And even if it does, you've still offered that person clarity they can use, a perspective they didn't have, and a chance to make a better choice. And there's a good chance that will be remembered as care.

When Truth Requires Showing, Not Telling

Words can be protective, redemptive, and transformative, but they aren't always enough. Sometimes truth requires helping someone see for themselves.

Frances Perkins understood this. Before she transformed American labor policy as FDR's secretary of labor, the first woman to serve in a presidential cabinet, she was a social worker in New York who witnessed the Triangle Shirtwaist Factory fire of 1911.[60] She watched 146 garment workers, mostly young immigrant women, die because the factory owners had locked the exit doors to prevent theft and unauthorized breaks.

That moment transformed her. She dedicated her life to worker safety and labor rights. But she learned something crucial in those early years: politicians who hadn't seen suffering firsthand simply couldn't understand the urgency of addressing it. No amount of reports, statistics, or passionate speeches could create the understanding that direct experience provided.

So when she needed President Roosevelt to understand the reality of working conditions in America, she didn't schedule a meeting in the Oval Office. She took him to see the slums personally. She brought him face-to-face with the poverty and suffering that his policies needed to address. The truth she needed him to grasp couldn't be transmitted through words. It required his presence, his senses, his direct experience of what working people faced.

Remember in chapter 8 when I told you to stop offering and start doing? Sometimes the most powerful form of truth isn't a message delivered. It's an experience created. Frances Perkins stopped trying to tell Roosevelt about poverty. She showed him instead. Because some truths only land when they're lived. When words fall short, invite people into the reality you want them to understand. Let them see the strain, the beauty, the harm, the possibility with their own eyes. Experiences cut through defensiveness, inertia, and abstraction. They make truth undeniable.

Truth to the Many

Not all truth moments happen one-on-one. Sometimes you have to deliver hard truth to an entire organization at once.

In 2009, with the Great Recession crushing our mortgage-industry clients, I faced one of the hardest truth moments of my career. Our revenue had cratered. Clients were declaring bankruptcy. The math on my glass office walls told a story I didn't want to believe. We were running out of options.

I gathered everyone together and told them the truth: every single person in the company, including me, needed to take a 30-percent salary reduction. No exceptions. Not temporary. Not for a few weeks. Until we survived this thing.

I could have laid people off instead. That's what most CEOs were doing. Cut 30 percent of your staff, keep the survivors at full salary. It's cleaner on paper. The remaining employees feel grateful to still have jobs, and you don't have to look everyone in the eye and ask them to sacrifice.

But I'd learned something from the companies I admired: you don't throw people overboard when the storm hits. You ask everyone to bail water. We were all in this together. We would all survive together or fail together. The truth I delivered wasn't just about the salary cut. It was about who we were as an organization.

The shared sacrifice created a bond that years of pizza parties and team-building exercises never could have. We weren't just colleagues anymore. We were survivors of the same storm.

That's the thing about truth-telling: the principles don't change when the audience gets bigger. Whether you're sitting across from one person or standing in front of a hundred, people respond to the same things: clarity, honesty, and a sense that you're in it with them.

When you tell the truth to many, you're still inviting them into a reality you need them to see. You're still asking them to live the hard facts with you, not just hear them. And when people share an experience of truth, its weight and its cost and its purpose, it binds them together in a way no memo or speech ever could.

Truth scales. Integrity scales. Shared reality scales.

And when you speak truth to a group, you're not just communicating information. You're shaping a collective identity. You're giving people something to hold onto. Together.

The Truths We Cannot Name

On a trip to Portugal, I spent my evenings in small bars where local musicians performed fado, the traditional music of the country. Night after night, I sat listening to the most haunting, beautiful music I'd ever heard. The singers were mostly women: mothers, daughters, sisters. And they were singing about a word I'd never encountered before.

Saudade.

The word describes a deep, nostalgic longing to be near again to someone or something that is distant or that has been loved and then lost. It's the love that remains when the person is gone.[61]

What fascinated me was the context. These songs emerged from a specific historical moment. Portugal was a seafaring nation. Men got on ships for work, sailing to distant lands to find fortune or simply to survive. And the women they left behind faced three possible fates, all unknown.

The ship could crash. Everyone could perish. The women waiting at home would never know what happened. Their husbands, fathers, sons simply would never return, and no explanation would ever come.

Or the ship could land in a new world, and whether by choice or circumstance, their loved one could decide to stay. Make a new life. Never come home. And again, the women would never know. Did he die? Did he choose to leave us? The uncertainty would last forever.

Or he could return at some unknown time, and they would be reunited. But when? Next month? Next year?

So many of these women spent their lives in a state of longing and limbo. And fado gave voice to that experience. Song after song, incredible women singers poured their hearts out about a moment they wanted so badly, a reunion that might never come.

I found the concept fascinating. It's not a word we have in English. It's not an event or emotion I would have ever thought to have a word for. And yet here was an entire musical tradition built around naming this specific form of truth.

This led me to a realization: not all truths have words in our language. Different cultures have developed vocabularies for emotional experiences that we feel but cannot name.

Onsra from the Boro language of India means to love for the last time, with the painful awareness that it cannot last. *Tu'burni* in Arabic translates roughly to "I love you so much that I hope I die before you, because I couldn't bear to live without you." *Mamihlapinatapai* from the Yaghan language of Chile describes a shared look between two people, each hoping the other will begin something they both want but are too hesitant to start.[62]

These words remind us that truth exists beyond our ability to articulate it. Sometimes the most important truths in our lives are ones we're feeling but have no vocabulary for yet.

Systematizing Truth: How Are You Leaving?

Truth doesn't have to be a dramatic event. It can be a practice woven into the fabric of how you work.

At PeopleG2, we developed an exercise we called "bonding" that happened several times a week within each team. At the end of meetings, we'd go around and ask everyone one simple question: "How are you leaving?"

Not, "How was the meeting?" Not, "Any questions?" "How are you leaving?"

This created space for hard truths that would otherwise go unspoken. Someone might say, "Confused," and we'd immediately know we needed to clarify something before sending them back to their work. Someone might say, "Unsure," and we'd explore what was creating that uncertainty. Someone might say, "Excited," and we'd know we'd hit on something important.

The genius of the exercise was that it gave structured permission for honesty. In most meetings, people nod along even when they're lost. They say, "Sounds good," when they're actually worried. They leave confused and struggle at their desks instead of speaking up. The "How are you leaving?" question interrupted that pattern. It made truth-telling normal, expected, routine.

This is what Amy Edmondson means by "psychological safety." Not the absence of conflict but the presence of permission. Permission to say what's really happening. Permission to admit confusion without being judged. Permission to speak truth without fear.

The Diagnostic: Where Truth Fails

Truth moments also have predictable failure patterns. Perhaps you recognize yourself in one or more of the following:

- **Identification Failure.** If you can't identify truth moments, you're probably avoiding discomfort. The conversation that needs to happen keeps getting pushed to next week. The feedback that could transform someone's career stays locked in your head because delivering it would be awkward. You tell yourself you're being kind by not saying anything, but you're actually operating in Ruinous Empathy. The truth is there. You just don't want to look at it.

- **Commitment Failure.** If you can't show up in truth moments, you're probably softening the message until it's meaningless. "Have you considered maybe, possibly thinking about perhaps adjusting your approach slightly?" That's not truth. That's politeness disguised as feedback. By the time you've qualified and hedged and cushioned the message, the recipient has no idea what you actually mean. They leave the conversation thinking everything is fine.

- **Narrative Failure.** Part of building a successful narrative is continuity. If you can't leverage truth moments, you're probably delivering truth without follow-up support. You drop the bomb and walk away. You tell someone that they need to change but provide no pathway for how that change might happen. Truth without support is just criticism. Carrie came back to PeopleG2 because she knew she'd have support in implementing what she'd learned. Truth creates possibility. Follow-up transforms that possibility into reality.

The Truth Moment Tool Kit

To practice more caring and effective truth-telling, try the following:

- **The Safety Setup.** Before delivering hard truth, establish explicitly why you're doing it. "I'm sharing this because I care about your success," or "I'm telling you this because I believe you can handle it and grow from it." Remember: Radical Candor involves the right balance of care and challenge. Demonstrate that with your words.

- **The Third Space Protocol.** Before any truth moment, take time to prepare your nervous system. Breathe. Center yourself. For truth moments, the Third Space means preparing not just your words but also your presence. Anticipate reactions and prepare to hold space for them without becoming defensive.

- **Attack Behaviors, Not People.** This principle from chapter 5 also applies in truth moments. "Your work on this project fell short of standards" is different from "You're not good enough." The first addresses behavior that can change. The second attacks identity, which creates defensiveness and shame rather than growth. Choose the former and avoid the latter.

- **Stay Regulated When They Dysregulate.** When you deliver hard truth, the other person may become emotional. They may cry, get angry, shut down, or storm out. Your job is to stay regulated. Don't escalate. Don't retreat. Just stay present and calm. Your nervous system regulation can help theirs return to baseline.

- **The Eighteen-Month Rule.** Remember that initial reactions aren't final verdicts. The truth you deliver today may take months to fully land. It took a full eighteen months before Carrie had digested the truth I gave her, so use that number as a frame of reference. Don't give up on the impact of your truth just because the first reaction wasn't what you hoped for.

The Gift of Being Told

I think often about James Meyers and that moment at ABL when he told me I might not be the right CEO of my own company.

If he had softened the message, I wouldn't have heard it. If he had qualified it into oblivion, it wouldn't have echoed in my head for months. If he had been "nice" instead of truthful, I might never have evolved into the leader PeopleG2 needed.

Truth delivered with care is a gift. Not everyone will receive it. Or they may not receive it right away. Carrie needed eighteen months. I needed three. Becky might never have received

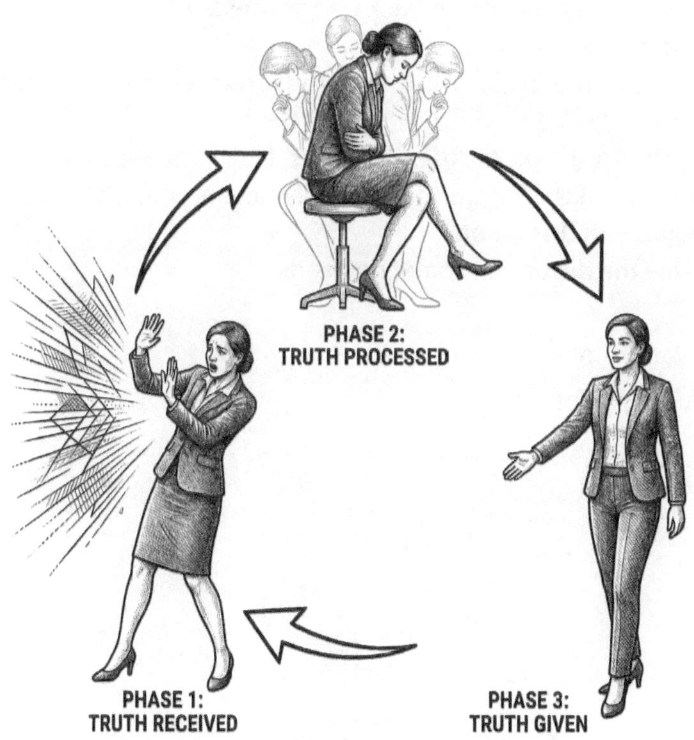

Figure 9.1. The truth cycle: received, processed, given.

the truth that her boyfriend was bad news even if I had spoken up.

But the possibility of rejection doesn't excuse us from offering the gift.

Sometimes truth requires dramatic reframing. Sometimes it requires physical demonstration. Sometimes it requires the courage to say something that might end a relationship.

The question isn't whether your truth will be received. That's not in your control. The question is whether you'll offer it: prepared, with care, for their benefit, with full release of the outcome.

Your people are waiting for truths they haven't heard yet. Some of them will cry. Some will quit. Some will need months or years to process what you tell them.

And some will come back transformed, ready to offer the same gift to others.

That's the cycle. Truth received. Truth processed. Truth given.

The truth will set them free. But first, it might piss them off. That's okay. Transformation rarely begins with gratitude. It begins with disruption.

Be the disruption someone needs.

"Every new beginning comes from some other beginning's end."
SENECA

CHAPTER 10

CULMINATION MOMENTS: ENDINGS THAT BECOME ORIGINS

The strange thing about endings is that they never feel like endings when you're experiencing them. They feel like Tuesdays. Like another phone call. Like one more signature on one more document.

On December 31, 2021, I stepped outside a New Year's Eve dinner to sign the final documents transferring ownership of PeopleG2, the company I'd built over twenty years. The deal closed virtually, which felt fitting for a company that had been remote since 2009. I used my finger to scrawl my signature on an iPhone screen, hit send, and stood there in the cold for a moment, waiting for something to happen.

Nothing did.

I went back inside, rejoined the dinner, and pretended everything was normal. My wife knew. A few close friends knew. But the moment itself felt anticlimactic, almost embarrassingly small for something that was supposed to be the culmination of my life's work.

The signing was supposed to be a triumph. Instead, it launched an identity crisis that lasted the better part of a year. Not because anything went wrong with the sale but because I'd failed to recognize what I was ending. I treated the culmination like a transaction instead of a transformation.

What I didn't understand then, what would take me months to fully grasp, is that culmination moments only become origins when you honor them as endings first. Most of us rush

Figure 10.1. Endings that become origins.

past endings to get to the next beginning. We treat culmination as a formality, a box to check before moving on. But the seed of what comes next is planted in how you complete what came before.

The Greatest Man in the World

On an even more momentous December day in 1783, George Washington walked into the Maryland State House in Annapolis to do something no conquering general had done since Cincinnatus in ancient Rome: voluntarily surrender absolute power.

The room was packed. Delegates, dignitaries, and citizens had crowded into the chamber, many standing along the walls. The Continental Congress sat waiting, unsure what exactly they were about to witness. Washington had defeated the most powerful military in the world. His army was fiercely loyal. The new nation had no real government, no stable currency, no functioning institutions. If any man in history had earned the right to seize power, it was Washington. If any moment invited a coup, it was this one.

He had arrived in Annapolis four days earlier, on December 19. The Continental Congress, then America's only governing body, was meeting in the city temporarily. Washington knew what he was going to do. He had thought about little else for months. The war was finally over. The Treaty of Paris had been signed in September. The last British troops had evacuated New York City on November 25. Everything was concluded except one final act.

Across the Atlantic, King George III had heard rumors of what Washington was planning to do. When the American-born painter Benjamin West told him that Washington intended to resign his commission and return to private life, the King reportedly said, "If he does that, he will be the greatest man in the world."[63]

The King understood what was at stake. Every revolution in history had ended the same way: the general who won the war became the ruler who seized power. Cromwell in England. Caesar in Rome. This was the pattern, the expectation, the inevitable conclusion to every successful rebellion. Washington's officers had even written to him suggesting he become America's king. He had rejected the idea emphatically, but the offer itself revealed what everyone assumed would happen.

The night before his resignation, Congress honored Washington with a feast at Mann's Tavern. Between 200 and 300 guests attended. Later that evening, Maryland Governor William Paca held a ball in Washington's honor at the State House. Nearly 600 people came. Washington, famously skilled on the dance floor, spent the evening dancing the minuet, astonishing French officers with his grace and skill. It was a celebration, but it was also a farewell.[64]

At noon the next day, Washington entered the chamber dressed in his Continental Army uniform. His hands trembled as he pulled out his prepared remarks. Those who witnessed the scene later described it as one of the most emotional moments they had ever experienced. David Howell, a delegate from Rhode Island, wrote of "a most copious shedding of tears." James McHenry, another witness, noted that Washington's voice "faltered and sunk" as he read.[65]

His speech was short. Just a few hundred words. But in those words, Washington did something that would shape American democracy for centuries: he demonstrated that power could be given up willingly.

"Having now finished the work assigned me," Washington read, his voice wavering, "I retire from the great theater of action; and bidding an affectionate farewell to this august body under whose orders I have so long acted, I here offer my commission and take my leave of all the employments of public life."

Then he handed over his commission, bowed, and left.

The next day, Christmas Eve, he rode home to Mount Vernon. He had promised his wife, Martha, he would be there by Christmas morning. He kept his promise.

What made Washington's culmination moment so powerful wasn't just that he walked away from power. It was how he walked away. He didn't sneak out. He didn't delegate the resignation to a subordinate. He didn't minimize the moment or rush through it. He stood before the people he'd led, allowed himself to be emotionally overwhelmed, spoke directly about what was ending, and then physically handed over the symbol of his authority.

Washington understood something most of us miss: Endings require ceremony. They require witness. They require the full weight of your presence, even when your voice is shaking and tears are streaming down your face.

And because he honored the ending so completely, it became an origin. Not just for Washington, who would return six years later to become the nation's first president, but for the entire American experiment. His resignation established the precedent of civilian control of the military. It demonstrated that leaders could serve and then step aside. It created the expectation that power in this new nation would be held temporarily, not seized permanently.

The ending became an origin because Washington refused to rush past it.

The Science of Endings

Psychologist Daniel Kahneman, who won the Nobel Prize for his work on judgment and decision-making, discovered something counterintuitive about how we remember experiences. In one trial of a 1993 study, participants submerged their hands in painfully cold water for sixty seconds. In another trial, they kept their hands in the same cold water for sixty seconds, then endured an additional thirty seconds while the temperature was raised by just one degree.

Logic says people should prefer the shorter, less painful experience. But when asked which trial they wanted to repeat, participants chose the longer one. The slightly less painful ending made the entire ninety-second ordeal feel more tolerable than the sixty-second version.

Kahneman called this the peak-end rule: we judge experiences primarily by how we feel at their most intense moment (the peak) and how they end. The duration of the experience barely matters. A wonderful vacation with a terrible last day will be remembered as a terrible vacation. A challenging project with a triumphant finale will be remembered as a great success.[66]

Kahneman and his colleague Barbara Fredrickson described this as the difference between our "experiencing self" and our "remembering self." The experiencing self lives through every moment. The remembering self creates the story we tell about what happened. And the remembering self doesn't average all the moments together. It focuses on peaks and endings.

This research reveals something profound about culmination moments: they're not just the last thing that happens. They're often the determining factor in how we remember everything that preceded them.

Washington's resignation became the defining story of his military career. Not the crossing of the Delaware. Not the winter at Valley Forge. Not even his army's victory at Yorktown. The ending is what we remember, what we teach, what we celebrate.

The peak-end rule explains why so many leaders fail at culmination moments. We spend enormous energy on beginnings. We celebrate launches, kickoffs, inaugurations. We plan first days with obsessive detail. But endings? We let them happen to us. We let them fade instead of finish.

And in doing so, we squander the moment that will determine how everything else is remembered.

The Dream That Died So Something Better Could Live

In high school and into college, water polo was everything to me. I was good. Better than good. I made the Junior Olympic team. The trajectory was clear: Olympic training, national team, maybe eventually the Olympics themselves. Every early morning practice, every afternoon drill, every weekend tournament was building toward that destination. The smell of chlorine was the smell of my future.

Then came the injury.

I don't remember the exact moment it happened, unlike the way you remember a car crash or a fall. It was more gradual than that, a problem that kept getting worse until one day a doctor told me what I already knew: my competitive playing career was over, as I had torn my groin muscle. The Olympic dream was gone.

At the time, this felt like failure. Not a culmination but a termination. Something that was supposed to continue had been cut short. I grieved that loss for months, maybe longer. The pool, which had been my sanctuary, became a reminder of what I'd lost.

What I couldn't see then was that the ending of my playing career was creating space for something I never would have discovered otherwise. Because I could no longer play, I started coaching. While still in college, I went back to the high school where I'd distinguished myself as the MVP and began working with the water polo and swim teams.

Coaching was different. In competition, you're focused on your own performance, your own body, your own moment. But coaching is about everyone else. You watch, you adjust, you figure out how to help each person become better than they thought they could be. You see patterns that players can't see themselves. You become a mirror that reflects potential back to people who can't see it on their own.

Coaching helped me develop skills of observation, of developing others, of having difficult conversations that lead to growth. I discovered that I was good at reading people quickly, at identifying potential, at helping individuals figure out how to become better versions of themselves. These abilities became the foundation for my career in human resources and eventually for leading PeopleG2.

Over the years, I've thought about this a lot. If I'd made the Olympic team, I would have touched maybe a few hundred lives directly: other players, coaches, fans who followed the sport. But coaching opened a door to a different kind of impact. I'd go on to play a role in the lives of thousands of employees and clients and the communities they served.

The injury that felt like a termination was actually a culmination. My Olympic dream ended so that something far greater could begin.

I couldn't see it at the time. You rarely can. The seed of what comes next is often invisible, buried in the soil of what's ending. It only sprouts later, when you've stopped mourning what you lost long enough to notice what you've gained.

Being Fired Became the Best Thing

In June 2005, Steve Jobs stood before the graduating class of Stanford University and told them about three stories from his life. The second story was about love and loss.[67]

"I was lucky," Jobs said. "I found what I loved to do early in life. Woz and I started Apple in my parents' garage when I was twenty. We worked hard, and in ten years, Apple had grown from just the two of us in a garage into a $2 billion company with over 4,000 employees. We had just released our finest creation, the Macintosh, a year earlier, and I had just turned thirty. And then I got fired."

The students laughed nervously. Jobs continued.

"How can you get fired from a company you started? Well, as Apple grew, we hired someone who I thought was very talented to run the company with me, and for the first year or so, things went well. But then our visions of the future began to diverge, and eventually, we had a falling out. When we did, our board of directors sided with him. So at thirty, I was out. And very publicly out."

Jobs described feeling devastated. Everything he'd built was gone. He'd failed publicly and spectacularly. For a few months, he didn't know what to do with himself.

"But something slowly began to dawn on me," he told the graduates. "I still loved what I did. The turn of events at Apple had not changed that one bit. I had been rejected, but I was still in love. And so I decided to start over."

What followed was what Jobs called the most creative period of his life. He founded NeXT, a computer company that would eventually be acquired by Apple and become the foundation of every Mac, iPhone, and iPad. He bought a small animation company from George Lucas and nurtured it into Pixar, which would revolutionize filmmaking and eventually be acquired by Disney for $7.4 billion. He met his wife and started a family.

"I'm pretty sure none of this would have happened if I hadn't been fired from Apple," Jobs admitted. "It was awful-tasting medicine, but I guess the patient needed it."

Jobs ended the speech with a story about *The Whole Earth Catalog*, a publication he'd loved as a young man. On the back cover of the final issue, the one that marked the catalog's own culmination, was a photograph of an early morning country road, the kind you might find yourself hitchhiking down if you were so adventurous. Beneath it were the words "Stay hungry. Stay foolish."

"It was their farewell message as they signed off," Jobs told the students. "Stay hungry. Stay foolish. And I have always wished that for myself. And now, as you graduate to begin anew, I wish that for you."

Jobs understood what I would later learn about culmination moments: the ending of one story is never really an ending. It's the opening line of the next chapter. But you have to be willing to close the book you're holding before you can pick up the new one.

The Captain's Last Swing

Sports provide some of the clearest examples of culmination moments because, unlike the rest of life, they have defined endings. Games end. Seasons end. Careers end. And once in a blue moon, those endings become legendary.

On September 25, 2014, Derek Jeter played his final game at Yankee Stadium. For twenty years, he had been "The Captain," the shortstop who'd led the Yankees to five World Series championships. He was forty years old, his body breaking down, his batting average hovering around .205. Everyone knew this was it.[68]

The Yankees had a plan. After the game ended, Jeter's former star teammates Mariano Rivera, Jorge Posada, Andy Pettitte, Bernie Williams, and Tino Martinez, along with their old manager Joe Torre, were waiting in the tunnel. They would lead Jeter on a victory lap around the stadium, a ceremonial farewell from the legends to the legend.

The game was supposed to end routinely. The Yankees had a three-run lead in the ninth inning. David Robertson, their closer, just needed three outs. Easy. Safe. Predictable.

But the Baltimore Orioles had other ideas. Adam Jones hit a two-run homer. Then Steve Pearce hit a game-tying solo shot. Suddenly, the game was tied at five going to the bottom of the ninth.

Jeter was due up third.

Later, he would admit he almost started crying driving to the stadium that day. That he had to retreat to the clubhouse during the game to compose himself. That he was so nervous in the field he hoped the ball wouldn't be hit to him. In fact, the first time he fielded a ball that night, he made a throwing error.

"I've done a pretty good job of controlling my emotions throughout my career," Jeter admitted after the game. "I have them; I try to hide them; I try to trick myself and convince myself that I'm not feeling those particular emotions."

But that night, he couldn't hide them. And he didn't try.

José Pirela led off the bottom of the ninth with a single. Brett Gardner bunted him to second. And there was Jeter, stepping into the batter's box for what everyone knew would be his final home at-bat.

The first pitch came in. An eighty-six-mile-per-hour changeup. Jeter swung with that trademark inside-out motion he'd used his entire career and slapped the ball through the right side of the infield. The runner scored. The Yankees won. And Yankee Stadium exploded.

Jeter, normally stoic and controlled, threw his hands in the air and let out a huge smile. His teammates mobbed him on the field. The crowd refused to stop cheering. The broadcast announcer fell silent, letting the moment speak for itself.

You cannot write scripts like this. That's what everyone said afterward. And they were right. You can't write them. But you can show up for them. You can be present enough, prepared enough, emotionally available enough to meet the moment when it comes.

The peak-end rule tells us that this single swing, this one moment, would now define how millions of people remembered Jeter's entire twenty-year career. Not the five World Series rings. Not the 3,465 career hits. This at-bat. This ending.

What I noticed watching the replays was that Jeter had been present for his own culmination the entire day. He let himself feel the emotion. He didn't try to control it or minimize it or rush past it. He showed up shaking and tearful and nervous, but he showed up just the same.

The ending honored the journey because Jeter honored the ending.

Unfinished Endings

Not all endings resolve. Some losses stay open forever. And sometimes the most important thing about a culmination moment is simply naming what we feel.

We are conditioned to believe that endings should make sense. Pain should soften into wisdom. Grief should eventually transform into gratitude. Every door closing should point us toward another one opening. But that isn't how many endings actually work. Some arrive without explanation. Some leave without apology. Some never tell us what they meant or what they were for.

There are moments when life doesn't offer closure, only absence. The employee who dies before retirement. The relationship that ends without resolution. The parent you never got to thank before they were gone. The words you never said because you assumed there would always be more time. These endings don't become origins in any obvious way. They don't lead to new companies or new careers or standing ovations. They just stay with you, an ache that never fully heals, a door that never really closes.

Across cultures, people have long understood this kind of unresolved ending, even when they haven't agreed on how to explain it. Languages all over the world contain words for emotions that don't neatly convert into English: feelings that mix love and loss, hope and resignation, longing and restraint. The very existence of these words tells us something important: Humans have always known that some emotional states can't be fixed. Only held.

When an ending refuses to resolve, our instinct is often to rush past it. To reframe it. To extract a lesson and move on. But sometimes the most honest response is to stop trying to repair what cannot be repaired. To resist the urge to make meaning too quickly. To allow the ending to remain incomplete.

And maybe that's okay. Maybe some culmination moments aren't meant to become beginnings. Maybe sometimes the most we can do is name what we feel, find the word that holds the weight of it, and let that naming be its own form of honoring the ending.

Not all endings resolve. But naming them truthfully, patiently, can still be an act of respect. And sometimes, that is enough.

What I Got Wrong

I told you earlier about signing those documents on New Year's Eve, the anticlimactic close of a twenty-year chapter. What I didn't tell you is what I should have done differently.

The sale itself went well. My employees were taken care of. Everyone received bonuses. Jobs were secure. The acquiring company was a good fit. On paper, this was exactly the kind of ending every entrepreneur hopes for.

But I treated the culmination like a transaction instead of a transformation. I didn't gather my leadership team for a proper goodbye. I didn't walk through the offices one last time, even virtually, to say thank you to the spaces that had held so much of my life. I didn't write letters to the people who had built the company alongside me. I didn't create any ritual to mark my passage from founder to former founder.

I just signed and walked back to dinner.

As I've already told you, the months that followed were brutal. What I hadn't anticipated was how completely my sense of self would unravel once the role I'd occupied for decades disappeared. When your identity is built inside a shared mission, when your days, relationships, and sense of purpose are deeply intertwined with a collective endeavor, the ending isn't just professional. It's personal. What I lost wasn't only a title or a company but also the structure, community, and meaning that had quietly shaped who I was. It took time to understand that this kind of ending demands more than resilience. It demands recognition. Like George Washington, I wished I'd understood that true endings require intention, ceremony, and witnesses willing to stand with you as one chapter closes and another remains, for a time, undefined.

If I could do it again, I would have gathered everyone at PeopleG2 together, told them what they meant to me, and cried in front of them the way Washington cried in front of Congress. I would have honored the ending before I tried to rush into the next beginning. Because when you don't honor the ending, it follows you. The grief you don't process in the culmination moment surfaces later, usually at inconvenient times, in unexpected ways. The identity you don't consciously release keeps tugging at you, making it impossible to fully become who you're meant to be next.

This is what I mean when I say culmination moments only become origins when you honor them as endings first. You can't skip the grief. You can't bypass the letting go. The only way to the next beginning is through the full experience of the current ending.

Where You're Failing at Culmination

In my work with leaders and organizations, I've identified three common failure points with culmination moments:

1. **Identification Failure.** If you can't identify culmination moments, things fade instead of end. Projects taper off instead of concluding. Employees leave and nobody marks the departure. You confuse "ending" with "stopping." Endings are intentional. They have shape and ceremony and meaning. Stopping is just ceasing to do something. If your organization is full of things that stop but never end, you're bleeding the narrative power that culmination moments create.

2. **Commitment Failure.** When endings arrive, you rush through them to avoid the emotion. You delegate the

goodbye speech to someone else. You skip the retirement party because you're "too busy." You process the departure paperwork without ever looking the person in the eye and saying what they meant to you. Every shortcut through an ending costs you the opportunity to create a new origin.

3. **Narrative Failure.** Even when you identify and show up for culmination moments, you miss the story gift they offer. Washington didn't just resign; he created a mythology that guided the nation for centuries. Johnson & Johnson didn't just recall Tylenol; they told the story of that decision until it became the gold standard for crisis management. The culmination moment is only half the work. The other half is ensuring that the story of that ending propagates forward, becoming part of how people understand what's possible.

The Culmination Tool Kit

To create more successful culmination points and fully harness their power, try the following:

- **Design endings like launches.** We spend weeks preparing for first days, kickoffs, and grand openings. We spend almost no time preparing for last days, final meetings, and closings. Even out the ratio. Plan the ending of a project with the same care you bring to its beginning. Who needs to be there? What needs to be said? What ritual will mark the passage from "doing" to "done"?

- **Bring high-sensory presence to endings.** Washington's hands trembled. His voice broke. Jeter's eyes watered. Jobs choked up describing his own firing. The emotion of endings isn't a weakness to overcome; it's information to honor. Let yourself feel the weight of what's ending. Let others see you feel it. The vulnerability of a fully felt ending creates the conditions for an authentic beginning.

- **Name what's ending before reaching for what's beginning.** I tried to leap from "CEO" to "What's next?" without ever stopping to say, "I'm no longer a CEO." The unnamed ending haunted me for months. Before you can become something new, you have to consciously release what you were. Say it out loud or write it down: "This chapter is over." Naming the ending is what creates the space for the next story to begin.

- **Ask exit interview questions of yourself.** Before any major ending, answer these questions: "What am I most proud of from this chapter? What do I wish I had done differently? What will I carry forward? What am I leaving behind? Whom do I need to thank? Whom do I need to forgive? The answers become the bridge from the old story to the new one.

- **Trust the Third Space.** Between the ending and the beginning lies a space of transition. Don't rush through it. Use it. The identity crisis that follows a major culmination isn't a problem to solve. It's a necessary passage through the unknown. Stay in the Third Space long enough to discover who you're becoming rather than desperately grasping for who you used to be.

Honoring the End

I started this chapter telling you about a December night when I signed away twenty years of my life and felt nothing. What I've learned since then is that the feeling was there all along. I just wasn't willing to feel it. I treated the culmination like a formality because I was afraid of what honoring it would require: admitting that something I loved was over, grieving the loss of an identity I'd worn for two decades, sitting in the uncertainty of not knowing who I would be next.

The rushed ending delayed my beginning. Instead of processing the transition in that single night, I processed it over months of confusion and purposelessness. The ceremony I avoided came anyway, just distributed across sleepless nights and mid-afternoon panic attacks and moments of staring at my phone, hoping for a notification from a company that was no longer mine.

Washington's hands trembled because he understood the weight of what he was doing. Jeter's eyes watered because he'd given twenty years to a team and a stadium and a city, and that deserved tears. Jobs's voice broke when he talked about being fired because losing something you built changes you in ways that never fully heal.

The trembling, the tears, the catch in the voice. These aren't signs of weakness. They're signs that you're taking the moment as seriously as it deserves. Endings only become origins when you honor them as endings first.

What's ending in your life right now? What culmination are you rushing past because you're afraid of what feeling it would require? What ceremony are you skipping because you're "too busy" or "too professional" or too scared to admit that something meaningful is over?

The exit door is right in front of you. On the other side is the next chapter, the new beginning, the person you're becoming. But you can't sneak through that door. You can't tiptoe past the ending and pretend it didn't happen.

You have to walk through deliberately. You have to let your hands tremble. You have to say goodbye and mean it.

One way or another, the future will open for you. But only an ending fully felt can become a beginning fully lived. Give yourself the gift of a proper goodbye and greet, unburdened, whatever comes next.

PART THREE:
THE PLAYBOOK

YOUR MOMENT
MASTERY SYSTEM

"We don't see things as they are; we see them as we are."

ANAÏS NIN

CHAPTER 11

THE MOMENTS AUDIT: SEEING WHAT YOU'VE BEEN MISSING

Her name was Marisol, and she'd been my operations manager for six years. She worked from her home in Arizona, and I worked from mine in California. We talked on video calls multiple times a week. I thought I knew her pretty well.

The Monday after we hit our Q3 revenue target in 2017, I sent an email to the leadership team: "We did it. Great work, everyone!" Then I moved on to the next thing. There was always a next thing.

What I didn't find out until months later was that Marisol had worked every weekend for three consecutive months to make that number possible. She'd missed her daughter's quinceañera rehearsal. She'd canceled her anniversary dinner twice. She'd been at her desk until midnight more times than she could count, debugging systems and managing crises I never heard about because she handled them before they ever reached me.

This is one of the hidden costs of remote work. When your team is distributed, you don't see the exhaustion. You don't notice when someone's light is still on at 11 PM. You don't walk past their desk and catch the slumped shoulders, the dark circles, the thousand-yard stare of someone who's given everything and is running on empty. Exceptional remote employees, the ones who care deeply about reaching the goal, often don't know when to turn off. They don't set boundaries because they want to deliver. And because you can't see them, you assume everything is fine.

Marisol wasn't fine. And I had no idea.

She quit three months later. When I asked why, she said something that still keeps me up at night: "You hit the number. You never saw what it took to get there."

Years later, after I'd sold the company and had time to reflect on all the things I'd gotten wrong, I called her and apologized.

"You were right," I confessed to her. "I was so focused on outcomes that I stopped seeing the people creating them."

We talked for over an hour. She'd landed somewhere good and was thriving. She forgave me. But she also told me something I've never forgotten: "The thing is, Chris, you weren't a bad boss. You just weren't paying attention to the right things."

That conversation changed how I think about leadership. I hadn't been cruel or neglectful in any obvious way. I'd simply developed blind spots so consistent that I could have mapped them had I only known to look.

As leaders, we can all use occasional refreshers on how to do exactly that. Looking. So that we'll find the moments we've been missing before they become the moments we regret.

Why the Missed Moments Compound

The research on this is unambiguous and uncomfortable. In 2001, psychologist Roy Baumeister and his colleagues published a landmark paper with a title that summarizes decades of findings: "Bad Is Stronger Than Good." Their review of the literature found that negative events had more impact than positive ones did across virtually every domain they studied. Bad feedback affects us more than good feedback does. Bad experiences are remembered more vividly than good ones are. Bad impressions form faster and resist change longer than good impressions do.[69]

In chapter 7, I introduced John Gottman's research on the "magic ratio": the finding that stable, healthy relationships require at least five positive interactions for every negative one. Not one-to-one. Five-to-one. Below that threshold, relationships deteriorate regardless of how committed the partners seem. The same pattern shows up in workplace research: teams that thrive maintain roughly that same ratio of positive to negative interactions.

The implications for leadership extend beyond recognition. Every moment you miss, every opportunity that passes by unacknowledged, every time you send a quick email when you should have picked up the phone, these aren't neutral events. They're negative ones. And they require five positive interactions to offset.

Marisol didn't leave because I was terrible to her. She left because I'd accumulated a deficit of missed moments that no amount of future acknowledgment could repay. The times I should have asked how she was really doing and didn't. The sacrifices I should have seen and didn't. Each missed moment subtracted from our relationship, and I never deposited enough positive moments to make up the balance.

The Normalization of Blindness

On February 1, 2003, the Space Shuttle Columbia broke apart during reentry, killing all seven astronauts aboard. The investigation that followed revealed that NASA had been watching foam break off from the external tank and strike the shuttle for years. Mission after mission, engineers raised concerns. Reports were filed. Meetings were held.

Nothing changed.

The foam strikes had become normal. Expected. Background noise. The Columbia Accident Investigation Board's final report identified eight separate moments during the shuttle's final sixteen-day flight when someone could have recognized the danger, requested satellite imagery, changed what was coming. Eight moments that passed unrecognized because the organization had lost its ability to see them.[70]

Figure 11.1. The moments we miss.

The Board's conclusion still chills me: "NASA's organizational culture had as much to do with this accident as the foam [did]."

I share this not to compare business challenges to shuttle disasters. The stakes are different. But the pattern of organizational blindness? I've seen it in every company I've worked with. We normalize what should alarm us. We optimize what should be sacred. We rush past moments that matter because we've stopped recognizing them as moments at all.

Marisol's weekends had become foam strikes. Expected. Normal. Part of what it takes to hit the number. I'd normalized her sacrifice into invisibility.

The Company That Checked Every Box

A few years after losing Marisol, I was hired to consult for a mid-sized healthcare technology company. Their CEO, Darnell, had called me about a retention crisis. Good people were leaving. Engagement scores were dropping. He couldn't figure out why.

Darnell was sharp in a way that reminded me of the characters on the TV show *Veep*. He'd been a Princeton undergrad and top of his class at an Ivy League school, and he had the kind of quick-witted intelligence that could slice through a bad argument before you'd finished making it. He'd built something real, and he was genuinely confused about why it was leaking talent.

"We're doing everything right," he told me during our first call. "Competitive salaries. Great benefits. Flexible schedules. We just renovated our office space."

I spent my first week watching. Sitting in meetings. Walking the halls. Eating lunch in the break room. Having coffee with people at different levels. What I saw wasn't a toxic culture or bad leadership. The people genuinely liked each other. The work was meaningful. Darnell cared about his employees.

The problem was subtler. I watched a new employee's first day unfold: two hours with HR filling out paperwork, an employee handbook dropped on her desk, a brief introduction to her manager, who was running late for another meeting, and then nothing. She sat alone at her desk for most of the afternoon, reading documents on her computer, occasionally glancing around like she wasn't sure if anyone remembered she was there.

I watched a promotion announcement happen via email. The recipient found out she'd been promoted when a calendar invitation appeared for a meeting with her manager. No ceremony. No acknowledgment of the four years of work that had led to this moment. Just a calendar ping.

I sat through a performance review that both the manager and employee clearly wanted to be over as quickly as possible. Checkboxes filled. Rating assigned. "Any questions? No? Great, see you next quarter." The whole thing took eleven minutes.

When I presented my findings to Darnell, he looked at me with genuine confusion.

"We have onboarding," he said. "We have promotions. We have performance reviews. We're doing all those things."

"You're doing the activities," I told him. "But you're not creating the moments. You've optimized for efficiency where you should have been taking it hard."

He'd built an organization that checked every box but missed every moment. Given the 5:1 ratio, his company was running a massive deficit. All those neutral interactions were actually negative ones, and there weren't nearly enough positive deposits to offset them.

The Three Ways We Fail

Through part two of this book, I identified failure patterns for each of the seven moment types. When I mapped them against Darnell's company, against my failure with Marisol, against hundreds of organizations I've studied, three patterns emerged.

The first is an identification failure. You don't recognize moments when they're happening. You treat everything with equal weight, which means nothing gets the weight it deserves. This is the NASA foam problem. When everything is normal, you stop seeing the abnormal. Marisol's weekends were invisible to me because weekend work had become expected. The new employee sitting alone on her first day was invisible to Darnell's team because first days had become administrative processes.

The second is a commitment failure. You recognize that a moment is happening, but you don't bring your full presence to it. You're distracted by the next meeting, the last email, the thing you need to do after this. The person on the other side can feel the difference. They know they're getting the efficient version of you instead of the real one. That eleven-minute performance review wasn't a conversation. It was a transaction. Both people were physically present but emotionally elsewhere.

The third is a failure to create or leverage a narrative. You recognize the moment, you show up for it, but you don't amplify its impact afterward. You don't tell the story. You don't create the ritual. Research from McKinsey shows that moments can create what they call a "disproportionate uplift in experience," but only when organizations design systems to leverage them.[71] The moment alone isn't enough. The promotion that happened via email could have become a story the whole company told about what excellence looks like. Instead, it became a calendar notification that the recipient's teammates didn't even know about for a week.

Most organizations, most leaders, fail at all three. I certainly did. I didn't see Marisol's sacrifice. Even if I had, I probably would have thanked her quickly and moved on. And I definitely wouldn't have told the story of what she'd done in a way that made her contribution visible to the whole company.

The Moments Audit is designed to diagnose exactly where you're failing so you can start succeeding.

Running the Diagnostic

Performing a moments diagnostic means interrogating how, when, and how successfully you create or handle the seven types of moments outlined in part two. Look for weak points. Where are you struggling? What steps can you take to make those moments more meaningful?

When I ran this diagnostic on Darnell's company, the pattern was stark. Their inception moments, those crucial first impressions, had been optimized into paperwork. The new employee's first day was indistinguishable from getting a driver's license at the DMV. Their transition moments, the space between roles and identities, weren't being supported at all. People were handed new titles and expected to figure it out. Their recognition moments were inconsistent and delayed. Their truth moments, the performance reviews that should have been transformative conversations, had become eleven-minute box-checking exercises.

Darnell's company wasn't unusual. When I run this diagnostic with leadership teams, most discover the same thing: they're reasonably good at one or two moment types but failing at the rest. The failures aren't malicious. They're invisible. The moments have been normalized into processes that nobody questions anymore.

When I ran the diagnostic on myself after losing Marisol, the results were painful. I was decent at inception moments. I'd built elaborate welcome experiences for new employees. I was terrible at recognition moments. I recognized achievements, not sacrifice. I sent congratulatory emails while the humans who created those achievements sat exhausted at their home offices, wondering if anyone noticed what it had cost them.

I was also terrible at culmination moments. When people left the company, I'd do the exit interview, wish them well, and move on. A former employee once told me that her departure felt like "checking out of a hotel." She'd shared ten years of her life with me and my company, and I'd processed her exit like a transaction.

The diagnostic reveals the truth about where your attention actually goes versus where you think it goes. It's uncomfortable. It's supposed to be.

The Moment Inventory

Beyond the diagnostic, I recommend building what I call a Moment Inventory. This is a systematic mapping of every touchpoint in your organization where moments are either happening or should be happening.

When global research and advisory firm Gartner conducted research on employee experience, they found that less than one-third of employees felt that their HR teams understood their wants and needs.[72] The reason is simple: organizations haven't done the work of identifying which moments actually matter. They've built processes for every stage of the employee life cycle without ever asking which stages carry disproportionate weight.

Darnell's company discovered through this inventory that they had seventeen distinct touchpoints in their first-year employee experience. They'd designed intentional moments for three of them. Fourteen potential moments were happening by default.

The inventory maps your employee life cycle from first awareness through departure and beyond. That includes attraction and recruitment. The hiring decision. The offer and acceptance. The first day and first week. The first thirty and ninety days. Performance conversations. Recognition opportunities. Role changes and promotions. Difficult situations. Departures. Alumni relationships.

For each touchpoint, ask yourself these four questions: "What moment type is this?" "Is it designed or accidental?" "Who owns it?" and "What story is it creating?"

You don't need to turn every touchpoint into a production. That would violate my principle from chapter 2 about not inflating trivial moments. But you do need to know where your high-impact opportunities are so you can be intentional about taking them hard.

Future-Casting

The audit tells you where you are. Future-casting tells you when moments are coming.

If I'd been future-casting in the months before that Q3 target, I would have seen Marisol's sacrifice before it became invisible. Every Friday, I would have looked at my calendar and my team roster and asked, "Who's carrying a disproportionate load right now? Who's sacrificing something I haven't acknowledged? What moments are forming that I'm not seeing?"

In chapter 7, I introduced Future-Casting Fridays for recognition moments. The practice extends to all seven moment types. Every Friday, spend fifteen minutes with your calendar and your team roster. Ask yourself:

- "What inception moments are coming? Who's starting? What firsts are on the horizon?"

- "What transitions are in progress? Who's between roles, between projects, between phases of their career?"

- "What decisions are approaching? What choices will shape the next year?"

- "Who needs recognition? Not for what they've achieved but for who they are and what they're sacrificing?"

- "Where are connection opportunities? Whom haven't you really talked to?"

- "What truths need to be spoken? What conversation have you been avoiding?"

- "What's ending? What projects are wrapping up? Who's leaving?"

Future-casting is one way to take advantage of the Third Space. It creates the mental preparation that allows you to show up fully when moments arrive. You're not surprised by what's happening because you saw it coming.

The Amplification Questions

When you recognize a meaningful moment approaching, take a moment to reflect.

Before the moment happens, ask yourself, "Is this worth taking hard? Which of the seven moment types is it? If this goes well, what story will people tell about it?"

When the moment has passed, ask, "Did I show up fully? What story will be told? How should this be propagated?"

If I'd asked myself those questions when I noticed Marisol logging in on weekends, I would have realized something important was happening. That reflection might have looked like this:

Is this worth taking hard? Yes.

Which type of moment is it? Recognition.

If it goes well, what story will be told about it? The story of a leader who sees people, not just outcomes.

The questions create a feedback loop. Over time, you develop instincts. You start recognizing which moments matter before they arrive. You get better at showing up. You learn how to amplify impact.

What Happened to Darnell's Company

The audit revealed that Darnell's stated value, "People First," didn't match his organization's actual behavior. Every moment that should have been human had been optimized into something transactional.

His response was what separated him from leaders who hear feedback and do nothing. He sat with the discomfort. He didn't get defensive.

"We've been so focused on efficiency that we forgot why efficiency matters," he explained to his leadership team. "We were saving time on moments so we'd have time for what? More moments we rush through?"

Over six months, Darnell's company leadership redesigned their inception moments. New employees now had a first day that felt like an arrival, not a processing. They created rituals around transitions. Promotions became celebrations. They rebuilt performance conversations into actual conversations. They trained managers on connection. They established practices for endings that honored what came before.

The company's retention improved. Its engagement scores rose. But more importantly, something shifted in how people talked about working there. "I feel like this company sees me" became a refrain. Not from marketing materials. From exit interviews with candidates leaving competitors.

They'd started making deposits in the 5:1 account. The balance was finally moving in the right direction.

Your First Audit

Set aside one hour this week. Go through the seven moment types. For each, rate yourself: Can you identify it? Can you commit to it? Can you leverage it through a meaningful narrative?

Pick one weakness. Commit to improving it over the next thirty days. Run this quarterly.

The moments aren't missing. They're right there. You've just stopped seeing them.

Marisol taught me that.

For the complete Moments Audit worksheet and diagnostic tools, visit chrisdyer.com/moments.

"Design is not just what
it looks like and feels like.
Design is how it works."
STEVE JOBS

CHAPTER 12

DESIGNING MOMENTS: FROM ACCIDENTS TO ARCHITECTURE

In 1981, Scandinavian Airlines was dying. The company had lost $17 million the previous year. Employee morale had cratered. Passengers were fleeing to competitors. Industry analysts predicted bankruptcy within eighteen months.

Jan Carlzon became CEO that year. He was thirty-nine years old, relatively unknown, and walking into a disaster. His first act surprised everyone: He didn't cut routes. He didn't lay off staff. He didn't slash prices.

Instead, he started counting.

Scandinavian Airlines served roughly ten million passengers annually, with passengers encountering the airline approximately five times during a single journey: check-in, boarding, in-flight service, baggage claim, and occasional interactions in between. That meant the company had fifty million opportunities every year to create an impression.

Fifty million moments. Fifteen seconds each. That's all the time a frontline employee had to shape a passenger's perception of the entire airline.

Carlzon called these "moments of truth."[73] What made his insight invaluable was that he didn't just name them. He designed for them.

He flipped the organizational pyramid. Instead of frontline employees serving management, management would serve frontline employees. He gave gate agents authority to solve problems without supervisor approval. He trained staff not just

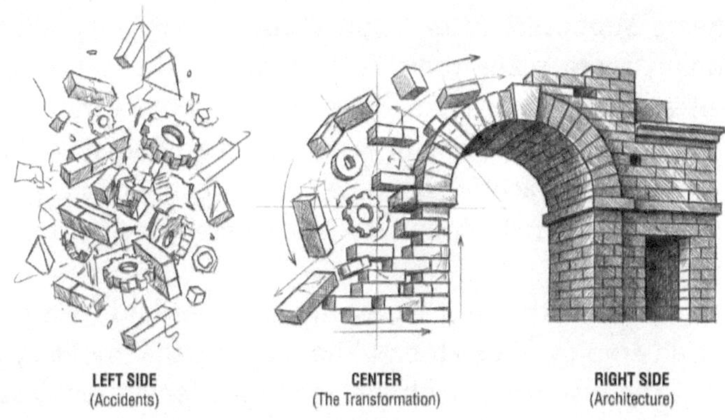

Figure 12.1. From accidents to architecture.

on procedures but also on reading situations, on recognizing when a passenger needed efficiency versus when they needed empathy.

Within one year, Scandinavian Airlines went from a $17 million loss to a $54 million profit. The American Management Association later recognized Carlzon's "moments of truth" concept as one of the most important management developments of the twentieth century.[74]

The moments hadn't changed. The passengers hadn't changed. What changed was intention. Carlzon took fifty million accidents and turned them into fifty million opportunities for design.

The Design Mindset

In part two, I walked you through seven types of moments that matter: Inception, Transition, Decision, Recognition, Connection, Truth, and Culmination. In chapter 11, the Moments Audit helped you diagnose where you're failing to identify, show up for, or leverage these moments.

Now comes the harder work: designing moments intentionally.

Most leaders I work with resist this idea at first. "Aren't moments supposed to be spontaneous?" they ask. "Won't designing them make them feel artificial?" The concern is understandable but misguided. Carlzon didn't make moments artificial by designing them. He made them possible. The design created space for genuine human connection. Without it, those fifty million opportunities were just fifty million transactions.

Think about the best experiences you've had as a customer, an employee, or a friend. The wedding that moved you to tears. The first day at a job that made you feel instantly valued. The conversation with a mentor that changed your trajectory. Behind every one of those moments was design, whether the designers themselves knew it or not. Someone chose the setting. Someone determined the timing. Someone prepared what they would say or do.

The question isn't whether to design moments. The question is how to design them well.

I learned how easily moment design can go wrong through a consulting engagement that still makes me cringe. A software company hired me to help improve their client relationships. Their renewal rates were solid but not spectacular, and they couldn't figure out why clients who seemed happy would suddenly switch to competitors.

"Our client satisfaction scores are great," the CEO told me in our first meeting. "Our NPS (net promoter score) is above industry average. But when contracts come up for renewal, we lose about 20 percent of accounts. It doesn't make sense."

When I shadowed the company's sales team, I found the problem immediately. Every time they closed a new contract, they celebrated by taking the client to an expensive steak dinner. There was champagne. Toasts. The works. The sales team loved it. They'd worked hard to close the deal, and this was their reward.

At those dinners, while the sales team celebrated, their clients looked uncomfortable.

I pulled one of those clients aside afterward and asked about the dinner. Her response was revealing: "It's nice, I guess. But we haven't done anything yet. We just signed a piece of paper. I'm nervous about whether this will actually work, and they're popping champagne like the hard part is over."

The company had designed a moment. They'd thought carefully about the timing, the setting, the experience. But they'd designed it entirely for themselves. The contract signing was their celebration. For the client, it was the beginning of uncertainty. They wanted a road map meeting, not a victory lap. They wanted reassurance, not champagne.

When I presented this to the leadership team, one executive pushed back. "But we're showing them we value the relationship," he professed.

"You're showing them you value winning," I replied. "That's not the same thing."

We moved the celebration to post-implementation. The client's first successful outcome became the moment. Same steak dinner. Same champagne. Completely different impact. Renewal rates jumped twelve points in a year.

The first principle of moment design is that the moment has to matter to the person it's for, not just the person creating it.

When Design Becomes Disaster

In 1997, Walmart entered Germany with supreme confidence. They were the world's largest retailer, the master of efficiency, the operator of over 8,500 stores in fifteen countries. They had a system that worked, and they were going to implement it. Why wouldn't it work? Retail is retail. Customers are customers. The same playbook that conquered America would surely conquer Europe.

Nine years later, Walmart abandoned the country with over $1 billion in losses. It wasn't a setback. It was a catastrophe. The company sold their eighty-five stores to a local competitor and left Germany permanently.[75]

What happened is a master class in designed moments gone catastrophically wrong. And the lessons apply far beyond retail.

Walmart had perfected the customer moment in America. Their playbook included mandatory employee smiles, enthusiastic greeters at every entrance, and a "ten-foot rule" requiring associates to smile at any customer within ten feet. They implemented the same playbook in Germany.

German customers found the smiling unnerving. "People found these things strange," a union secretary told reporters. "Germans just don't behave that way." Some male customers complained that the mandatory smiles felt like flirting. The warmth that worked in Arkansas felt fake and intrusive in Munich.

It got worse. Walmart required employees to start each shift with group stretching exercises and synchronized chants of "WALMART! WALMART! WALMART!" This practice, intended to build morale and loyalty, struck German workers as deeply embarrassing. Some found it reminiscent of a different kind of rally that had occurred in Germany decades earlier. The cultural tone-deafness was staggering.

Then came the ethics policy. Walmart prohibited romantic relationships between coworkers and required employees to report any rule violations by colleagues. In a culture that values privacy and solidarity among workers, this created intense resentment. A German court eventually struck down the policy in 2005, but the damage had been done.

Walmart had designed every moment meticulously. The greeting. The checkout experience. The employee rituals. They just hadn't asked a single question about whom those moments were actually for.

As one analyst put it, "Walmart essentially made proud Germans feel like colonized guinea pigs."

The lesson isn't that designed moments fail. The lesson is that designed moments without understanding fail spectacularly. Walmart didn't lack intention. They lacked humility. They assumed that what worked somewhere would work everywhere. They designed for themselves, not for the people they were trying to serve.

The Five Questions of Moment Design

Every moment worth designing requires the same five questions, in order:

1. **WHOM is this moment for?** Not who's creating it. Not who's observing it. Who is centered in this experience? The answer should be a specific person or type of person, not "everyone" or "the company." When Walmart designed their customer greeting, they answered this question with, "Walmart customers." They should have answered it with, "German shoppers who value personal space and distrust performative warmth."

2. **WHAT do you want them to feel, remember, and tell?** There are three different outcomes that need to align. What emotion should they experience in the moment? What should stick with them afterward? What story will they tell others? The steak dinner celebration made clients *feel* awkward. It made them *remember* that the company celebrated prematurely. And they would *tell* colleagues that the vendor seemed more interested in the sale than the outcome.

3. **WHEN does the moment need to happen?** This isn't just timing on a calendar. It's timing in the emotional arc of the experience. The celebration belonged after implementation, not after signature. Consider: What preparation needs

to happen before the moment that will lead to its success? How can I ensure my presence during the moment? What propagation should happen afterward?

4. **WHERE should the moment occur?** The physical and emotional setting matters more than most designers realize. A recognition moment in a crowded hallway feels different than one in a private office. A truth moment over lunch feels different than one in a conference room. The setting shapes what's possible.

5. **HOW will you know if it worked?** This is the question most organizations skip. If you can't measure it, you can't improve it. But measurement for moments isn't always quantitative. Sometimes it's observing body language. Sometimes it's hearing what stories get retold. Sometimes it's tracking downstream behavior changes.

These five questions form the foundation of intentional design. Skip any of them and you risk creating a Walmart Germany moment instead of a Carlzon moment.

Building on Research

In chapter 2, I introduced the work of Chip Heath and Dan Heath, whose research identified four elements that create powerful moments: elevation, insight, pride, and connection.[76] If these elements are the ingredients to a powerful moment, its design is the recipe. Knowing that elevation matters doesn't tell you how to create it for a specific person in a specific context. Knowing that insight transforms doesn't tell you when or how to deliver it. The gap between understanding and implementing is where most organizations fail.

Similarly, Daniel Kahneman's peak-end rule tells us that people judge experiences based on their most intense point and how they end.[77] But knowing this and designing for it are different skills. You have to identify where peaks should occur, what intensity they should reach, and how endings should feel for specific people in specific contexts. The peak in a recognition moment is different from the peak in a truth moment. The ending of an inception experience needs different qualities than the ending of a culmination.

My mentor Pete Sheahan pushed me on this distinction during one of our conversations. "The research tells you that peaks matter," he advised. "But it doesn't tell you that not everything should be a peak. Some things should just be normal. Some things should be efficient. The skill is knowing which is which."

He's right. One of the biggest mistakes I see organizations make is trying to turn everything into a moment. They create "moment fatigue" by treating every interaction as if it required the same level of intentional design. An email confirming a meeting time doesn't need to be a moment. A quick Slack message checking on a project deadline doesn't need to be a moment.

The Moments Audit from chapter 11 identifies which moments actually matter. Focus on designing those moments and leaving the others appropriately efficient.

Design Principles by Moment Type

Each of the seven moment types has specific design requirements. The five questions of moment design apply, but the answers differ:

Inception Moments center the question: "How do you want people to feel about who they're becoming?" The default to avoid is treating inception as onboarding paperwork. Take the PeopleG2 welcome packages from chapter 4, where we included Swedish Fish, personalized letters, and items from the new hire's questionnaire. The preparation reduced turnover from 35 percent to 12 percent because we designed for belonging, not processing.

Transition Moments center the question: "What does the space between require?" The default to avoid is skipping directly from the old identity to the new without honoring the passage. As I explored in chapter 5, transitions are the space where real change happens. Design should create room for that space, not rush past it.

Decision Moments center the question: "What would clarity look like?" The default to avoid is letting urgency compress the space for consideration. The 10-10-10 Rule from chapter 6 provides structure: How will this feel in ten minutes? Ten months? Ten years? Design should build in the pause that perspective requires.

Recognition Moments center the question: "What specifically am I seeing in this person?" The default to avoid is generic praise that could apply to anyone. Future-Casting Fridays from chapter 7 worked because the recognition was tied to specific observed behaviors and connected to concrete future implications.

Connection Moments center the question: "What does presence actually look like here?" The default to avoid is confusing proximity with connection. Being in the same room isn't connection. Being fully present is. Remember Papa Jack falling asleep while I was driving in chapter 8? Sometimes connection requires letting someone help you when you'd rather handle it yourself.

Truth Moments center the question: "How do I ensure that this lands as care, not criticism?" The default to avoid is delivering hard truths without considering how it will be received. Kim Scott's framework in chapter 9 matters here.[78] The truth has to come wrapped in genuine relationship and concern for the person's growth.

Culmination Moments center the question: "How do we honor what's ending before rushing to what's next?" The default to avoid is the "checking out of a hotel" departure from chapter 10. Endings that aren't honored become resentments that linger.

The Pre>In>Post Design Process

Moments that matter require work before, presence during, and action after. This framework applies to intentional design in specific ways:

Pre-Moment Design answers the question, "What preparation makes this moment possible?" At PeopleG2, I trained managers to think about moments before those moments arrived. Before a performance conversation, they'd ask, "What specific observations do I need to share? What does this person need to hear to grow? What story do I want them to tell themselves after we talk?" The preparation wasn't about scripting. It was about entering the moment with clarity and intention.

In-Moment Design answers the question, "What presence does this moment require?" This is where the Third Space Protocol from chapter 3 comes in. How do I clear whatever preceded this moment? How do I arrive fully? What does "taking it hard" look like for this specific situation? The design isn't about the words you'll say. It's about the state you'll be in.

Post-Moment Design answers the question, "How does this moment spread?" This is the propagation work. Do you tell the story? Create a ritual? Document what happened? Make the moment visible to others who weren't there? As I emphasized throughout part two, moments that aren't leveraged lose most of their potential impact.

When I ran PeopleG2, we made Pre>In>Post thinking part of manager training. Before any significant conversation, managers would answer three questions: "How will I prepare?" "How will I show up?" "How will I follow through?" Over time, this became instinctive.

That instinctive process becomes a way of moving through life more deliberately. When you learn to prepare with clarity, show up with your full self, and honor what happened once the moment has passed, ordinary interactions begin to carry extraordinary weight. This is how moments stop being accidental and start becoming meaningful, at work, at home, and everywhere in between.

The Authenticity Trap

Whenever I teach moment design, someone raises the same concern: "Isn't this just manufactured culture? Won't people see through it?"

This concern is legitimate. In a 2025 workplace study, 78 percent of employees said that culture matters to them, but not "manufactured culture."[79] Forty-two percent of Gen Z workers actively job searching cited lack of authenticity as a reason for seeking a better fit elsewhere. Forced celebrations breed resentment. Mandated fun backfires. People can smell inauthenticity from across the building.

Walmart's German disaster was manufactured culture. The smiling. The chanting. The elaborate policies designed to create a specific experience without any understanding of the people involved. Every designed moment felt forced because it was forced. The design happened *to* people, not *for* them.

But there's a crucial distinction between manufacturing moments and designing for them. It's the difference between a script and a stage.

Manufacturing tries to script the content. Designing creates the container. You can design a recognition ritual without scripting what people say. You can create space for transition without dictating what people feel. You can build the architecture for connection without controlling the connection itself.

The Swedish Fish in our welcome packages weren't manufactured warmth. They were a designed container for genuine personal touch. Every package was different because every person was different. The design was the system. The authenticity was what the system enabled.

When designing moments, focus on five elements of the container: the setting, the timing, the people present, the preparation, and the follow-up. Don't try to script what happens inside the container. That's where authenticity lives.

Common Design Failures

Beyond the cautionary tale of Walmart, I've cataloged patterns of moment design failures across organizations. And I've made most of these mistakes myself.

I once designed what I thought was a beautiful recognition moment for a team that had pulled off an impossible deadline. I planned the announcement for our company's all-hands meeting. I prepared remarks about their specific contributions. I even arranged for their manager to present custom awards.

What I didn't do was ask them how they wanted to be recognized.

Turns out that two of the four team members were deeply uncomfortable with public recognition. One later told me she spent the entire presentation trying not to cry from anxiety. Another said that he would have much preferred a quiet thank-you and a day off. I'd designed for the company and for my vision of what recognition should look like. I hadn't designed for the actual people I was trying to honor.

That experience taught me to look for these patterns:

- **Designing for yourself instead of the recipient.** It's the steak dinner celebration. Or the all-hands announcement that's really about leadership looking good. Or the recognition award that serves the company's PR more than the employee's growth.

- **Prioritizing production over person.** It's the elaborately planned event that becomes about the event, not the people in it. When the celebration serves the moment instead of the relationship, you've lost the plot.

- **Timing for convenience instead of impact.** It's the recognition that waits until the all-hands meeting because that's when leadership is available. Or the feedback that gets batched into quarterly reviews because that's when the system requires it.

- **One-size-fits-all design.** It's the assumption that what works for one person will work for everyone. Some people need public recognition; others find it mortifying. Some people need detailed feedback; others need the headline and time to process. The design has to flex for the recipient.

- **Inception without culmination.** It's organizations that design elaborate first-day experiences but treat departures as administrative processes. The imbalance is felt. People notice when their arrival was celebrated and their exit was processed.

- **No propagation plan.** It's the perfectly designed moment that nobody hears about because there was no intention to spread its impact. If the moment isn't leveraged, most of its value disappears.

What Excellence Looks Like

There's a fast-food chain in the Southeastern United States that makes a burger, fries, and a shake. There's nothing special about the menu but everything special about how they design every moment.

Pal's Sudden Service operates twenty-nine drive-through restaurants across Tennessee and Virginia. In 2001, they became the first restaurant company ever to win the Malcolm Baldrige National Quality Award, an honor previously reserved for such giants as Cadillac, FedEx, and Ritz-Carlton.[80] When President George W. Bush presented the award, founder Fred

"Pal" Barger said something revealing: "It's nice to have that recognition, but we didn't do all that for that."[81]

There's a noticeable difference between Pal's and Walmart, and it's that Pal's was designed for people. Recognition was a byproduct.

What makes Pal's noteworthy isn't its food. It's the restaurant chain's obsession with designing every customer interaction. A customer spends an average of eighteen seconds at the order window and twelve seconds at the pickup window. Competitors take over a minute at each. More striking is that Pal's makes a mistake only once every 3,600 orders. The industry average is one mistake every fifteen orders.

Pal's achieves this through relentless design. Every new employee goes through 120 hours of training before working independently. They're certified for each skill: cooking hamburgers, working the shake machine, taking orders. Every shift, a computer randomly selects employees to be recertified on specific skills. "It's our belief that human beings, just like machines, need to be recalibrated," CEO Thom Crosby noted.

One important point is that Pal's doesn't use speaker systems. Every order is made face-to-face. That eighteen-second window interaction isn't just faster than its competitors. It's designed as a human moment. There's eye contact. There's a smile that isn't mandated but emerges from genuine culture. There's a brief connection in the midst of efficiency.

When other business leaders ask Crosby about training investment, given high industry turnover, he has a standard response: "People ask, 'What if you spend all this time and money training someone and then they leave?' My answer is, 'Suppose we don't and then they stay?'"

Pal's turnover rate for hourly employees is one-third the industry average. Among managers, only seven have left voluntarily in three decades.

The company didn't just design moments. They designed systems that design moments. They built capability, not just playbooks. They created a culture in which moment design is embedded in how everyone thinks.

That's the difference between designing moments and becoming an organization that designs moments.

The Moment Architect's Tool Kit

I've developed a set of questions that I call the Moment Architect's Tool Kit. These questions create a feedback loop between identifying moments, designing them, and learning from them. Use them before, during, and after any moment that matters.

The tool kit works like a checklist for pilots. Pilots don't use a checklist because they don't know how to fly but because even experts forget things under pressure. Moments that matter create pressure. The tool kit ensures that you don't skip critical steps when stakes are high.

Identification Questions

Is this moment worth taking hard? (If efficiency is appropriate, let it be efficient.)

Which of the seven moment types is this? (Inception, Transition, Decision, Recognition, Connection, Truth, or Culmination?)

What story will be told if this goes well?

Design Questions

Who is centered in this moment?

What should they feel, remember, and tell?

What preparation does this require?

What setting enables the moment?

How will I know if it worked?

Propagation Questions

Did I show up with full presence?

What story is now being told?

How can this moment spread?

Who else needs to know what happened?

Use the Identification Questions before you commit design energy. Not every moment deserves it. Use the Design Questions to plan intentionally. Use the Propagation Questions to extend impact and learn for next time.

Over time, this becomes instinct. You start seeing moments before they happen. You develop intuition for what each moment requires. The questions become a habit of mind rather than a checklist.

The Hardest Part

Jan Carlzon transformed Scandinavian Airlines in a year. What most accounts of his success leave out is that the transformation almost collapsed eighteen months later.

I've seen this pattern dozens of times. A leader reads a book, attends a conference, or works with a consultant. They get inspired. They implement changes. The early results are promising. People are energized. Metrics improve.

Then month eighteen arrives.

The initial energy has faded. Old habits have reasserted themselves. Middle managers who had enthusiastically adopted the new approach have started reverting to familiar patterns. They're under pressure to hit quarterly numbers, and the careful moment design work has started to feel like a luxury they can't afford. Frontline employees who had been empowered have begun second-guessing their authority. The "moments of truth" that had been so carefully designed have started feeling like checkboxes again.

When Scandinavian Airlines yo-yoed into a second descent, Carlzon had to launch what he called a "second wave" of transformation, focused not on design but on sustainability. Not on creating moments but on maintaining the culture that enabled them. Not on the initial spark but on building systems that kept the fire burning.

This is where most moment design efforts fail. Not at the beginning, when energy is high and intention is fresh. At the eighteen-month mark, when novelty has worn off and competing priorities have emerged. When the designed moments start feeling routine and the old defaults look tempting. When the urgent crowds out the important.

McKinsey research confirms what Carlzon discovered: two-thirds of large-scale organizational transformations fail to meet expectations, and most of those failures happen not at launch but in sustainment.[82] The design works. The execution works. The momentum fades.

Pal's understands this. That's why it doesn't just train employees once. They recertify constantly. They embedded design into systems that renew themselves. They built infrastructure for moments, not just moments themselves.

The question isn't just, "How do I design this moment?" It's, "How do I build an organization in which moment design is perpetual?"

Carlzon didn't create fifty million new moments. He saw fifty million existing moments with new eyes and gave them intentional design. The moments were always there. The architecture wasn't.

Start small. Pick one moment type. Choose the one where your audit revealed the biggest gap. Design one moment intentionally and see what happens.

But remember that design alone isn't enough. The best-designed moments, executed once, disappear without reinforcement. The eighteen-month collapse waits for everyone who doesn't build infrastructure for renewal.

Design is where moments become intentional. Sustainability is where they become culture.

"We are what we
repeatedly do. Excellence,
then, is not an act, but a
habit."
ARISTOTLE

CHAPTER 13

SUSTAINING MOMENTUM: FROM PROJECT TO PERMANENT CAPABILITY

On March 28, 1842, a group of musicians gathered in Vienna's Imperial Opera Theater for what they called a "Philharmonic Academy." The conductor was Otto Nicolai. The program included works by Mozart and Beethoven. The audience was Vienna's cultural elite, dressed in silk and anticipation.[83]

Nothing about that evening suggested permanence. Vienna had no professional concert orchestra at the time. Musicians were assembled ad hoc for specific performances, then disbanded. This concert was an experiment, an aspiration, a bet that professional symphonic music deserved an institutional home.

Over 180 years later, the Vienna Philharmonic remains one of the most celebrated orchestras in the world.[84] They have performed continuously since that first concert. Not one year missed. Not during the revolutions of 1848. Not during either World War. Not during the Cold War or even COVID-19.

How does any organization sustain excellence for nearly two centuries?

The Vienna Philharmonic's answer contains lessons that apply far beyond music. Lessons about what makes moments sustainable instead of temporary, what transforms inspiration into institution.[85]

What makes them extraordinary isn't just that they've survived. It's that the group has sustained a distinctive sound, a particular way of playing that listeners can identify within

Figure 13.1. The four pillars of sustainability.

seconds. When you hear the Vienna Philharmonic, you know it's them. That consistency across nearly two centuries of personnel changes, leadership transitions, and cultural upheaval is what deserves examination.

My wife Jody and I caught one of their outdoor performances while visiting Vienna a few years ago. Hundreds of people gathered in the evening air, families with children, elderly couples, tourists like us who had stumbled onto something special. What I remember isn't the selections they played. I couldn't tell you the program. But I remember the timing, the warmth, the shared experience of strangers becoming a community for an hour. That's what over 180 years of sustained excellence creates. Not just technical mastery, but something that transcends the notes on the page.

The orchestra's sustainability teaches a principle I call Build for the Exit: creating something so embedded in infrastructure that it doesn't depend on you being there. The Vienna Philharmonic built for the exit through four elements: Systems, Stories, Symbols, and Succession. Let's consider each in turn.

Systems: Infrastructure for Moments

The Vienna Philharmonic uses instruments that most orchestras abandoned a century ago. Their timpani still use goatskin heads instead of synthetic materials. Their French horns are actually "Wiener horns," designed differently from modern instruments. The oboes, the brass, the strings all follow specifications that trace back to the orchestra's founding era.[86]

This isn't nostalgia or stubbornness. It's system design.

The instruments are owned by the orchestra, not the individual musicians. When a violinist joins the Vienna Philharmonic, they play on an instrument provided by the organization. When they leave, the instrument stays. The tools of moment making belong to the institution, not the individual. This ensures continuity regardless of personnel changes.

Beyond instruments, the Philharmonic operates through a system that would seem radical to most organizations: they have no permanent conductor. In 1933, they deliberately abandoned the model of having a single music director. Instead, they invite guest conductors for specific performances. The orchestra itself, through the democratic vote of its members, makes all key decisions about repertoire, conductors, and soloists.

Why would eliminating a leader improve sustainability? Because it prevents the organization's culture from becoming dependent on any single personality. The system is designed so that the institution, not the conductor, carries the sound.

I learned this lesson the hard way at PeopleG2. For twenty years, I was the center of gravity. Once I was gone, the culture that my former employees missed wasn't just the company's culture. It was culture filtered through me. When I left, that filter disappeared. The system wasn't designed for sustainability without me.

I'd treated my company like a family, and the truth is that families often lack the systems that enable sustainability. Think of the traditions that defined your childhood, the moments that shaped you as you grew into adulthood. Do they continue? Often they die with the generation that creates them. The holiday gatherings that meant everything to your grandparents become obligations their grandchildren skip. The weekly phone calls become monthly texts that become annual birthday messages. Without systems to sustain them, moments fade.

Systems are the infrastructure that makes moments repeatable. Without systems, every moment requires heroic effort. With systems, moments become organizational habit. The question isn't whether you need systems. It's whether you're designing them intentionally or letting them emerge accidentally.

The Vienna Philharmonic's instruments are one form of system. But systems can be simpler. Sometimes they're as basic as a price that never changes.

The Hot Dog Test

In 1984, Costco introduced a hot dog and soda combo at their San Diego warehouse. The price was $1.50.[87]

Forty-two years later, the price is still $1.50.

Accounting for inflation, that hot dog should cost about $4.75 today. Costco loses money on each one they sell. But their CFO has called the price "sacrosanct" and promised that it will remain fixed "forever." The story behind that commitment reveals everything about how Costco has sustained its culture through three CEO transitions in forty-plus years.

Craig Jelinek, who served as CEO from 2012 to 2024, once approached founder Jim Sinegal about raising the price.

"Jim, we can't sell this hot dog for a buck fifty," Jelinek implored him. "We are losing our rear ends."

Sinegal's response has become corporate legend: "If you raise the effing hot dog, I will kill you. Figure it out."[88]

That wasn't just colorful language. It was a system being transmitted. The hot dog represents Costco's core belief that you can build a profitable business while putting customers first. Every time a customer sees that $1.50 price, unchanged since Reagan's first term, they're experiencing a moment that says, "This company keeps its promises."

When Ron Vachris became CEO in January 2024, only the third person to hold that title in Costco's history, he was asked about the hot dog price. His answer: "Raising those prices will not happen on my watch."[89]

The system had been transmitted to the third generation.

But Costco's sustainability story got tested dramatically in early 2025. As company after company abandoned their diversity and inclusion commitments under political pressure, Costco's board faced a shareholder proposal demanding that they do the same. Major retailers had already capitulated. The pressure was intense.

Costco's board unanimously recommended that shareholders reject the proposal. Their statement was direct: "We're proud that Costco pays the highest wages among our peers, that we provide benefit and healthcare packages that are second to none, and that we've grown our business by promoting from within. Our commitment to inclusion has never included quotas or systematic preferences, nor does it mean compromising merit."[90]

Over 98 percent of shareholders voted with the board.

Ron Vachris, who started at Price Club (which merged with Costco in 1993) as a forklift driver in 1982 and spent forty-two years rising through the company, embodied what the vote affirmed: Costco's culture wasn't dependent on external validation or political winds. It was systematized into how they operate, whom they promote, and what they refuse to compromise on.[91]

Fast Company named Vachris their "Visionary of the Year" for 2025, noting that "his ascent is a testament to Costco's promote-from-within philosophy."[92] The philosophy became the system. The system created the culture. The culture is sustained through leadership transitions and external pressure.

That's what sustainable moments look like.

Stories: How Moments Become Memory

The Vienna Philharmonic maintains historical archives containing thousands of objects, letters, and photographs. Among them is a piano excerpt from Beethoven's opera *Fidelio*, one of only five copies known to exist in the world. Another treasure is a simple memo, almost unremarkable in appearance, containing the founding decree that Otto Nicolai wrote in 1842.

"It contains the most important principles that are still upheld by the Vienna Philharmonic today," explained the orchestra's archivist.[93]

Why preserve a memo for over 180 years? Because stories need artifacts. Moments need evidence. The founding document isn't just paper. It's proof that today's orchestra stands in direct continuity with its origins.

Science explains why stories matter so much. Neuroeconomist Paul Zak at Claremont Graduate University discovered that stories with dramatic arcs cause the brain to release oxytocin, the same chemical that bonds mothers to newborns. When Zak measured what happens after oxytocin release, he found something striking: people donate 56 percent more money and give to 57 percent more charities.[94]

Stories don't just make us feel connected. They change behavior. They make us act. This is why the Costco hot dog story works. It releases the brain chemistry that builds trust. And each retelling triggers the same neurochemical response, reinforcing the culture in a way that policy manuals never could.

Every organization that sustains its culture across generations does so through stories. Not mission statements hanging on walls. Stories that get told and retold until they become organizational DNA.

The Costco hot dog story has been told millions of times. Every article about the company mentions it. Every employee knows it. "If you raise the effing hot dog, I will kill you" isn't just a funny quote. It's a story that transmits values more effectively than any policy manual can.

In chapter 7, I told you about the All Blacks and their ritual of "sweeping the sheds," where the most senior players pick up brooms and clean the locker room after matches. What I didn't emphasize then is how that ritual became sustainable: through story. Former players tell new players. Coaches tell recruits. The story of Steve Hansen starting to sweep, and players joining in, and custodial staff being turned away, gets repeated until it becomes what it means to be an All Black.

At PeopleG2, we had stories too. The Texas power outage and the generators we bought for employees. The military spouse program. The holiday cards. But when I sold the company, those stories went with me. I didn't realize that stories need to be formally captured, documented, and ritually transmitted in order for them to survive leadership transitions.

The Vienna Philharmonic doesn't just keep archives. They have educational programs that teach the orchestra's history. They publish books. They create exhibitions. The stories aren't just preserved. They're propagated.

That's the difference between moments that fade and moments that last. Fading moments happen and end. Lasting moments get captured in stories, and those stories get told until they become what everyone knows without being taught.

Symbols: The Visible Reminders

Every New Year's Day, the Vienna Philharmonic performs a concert broadcast to over ninety million people worldwide. The program always includes works by Johann Strauss. The venue is always the Golden Hall of the Musikverein. The decorations always feature flowers from San Remo, Italy.[95]

The New Year's Concert is a symbol. It says, "We are still here. We are still performing. The tradition continues."

Symbols are moments made visible. They're the artifacts, rituals, and traditions that remind everyone, constantly, what the culture stands for.

Costco's $1.50 hot dog is a symbol. The unchanged price makes values tangible. Customers can see, taste, and experience what the company believes about keeping promises.

But symbols don't have to be corporate. They can be personal. They can be small.

Every summer, my wife Jody and I host a *biergarten* party at our home. It started in 2018, just a few couples, some German food, a keg of beer. Now it's grown to over 150 people. Musicians play. Kids run around. Friends who haven't seen each other all year catch up over bratwurst and pretzels.

In 2024, however, the Biergarten nearly died. Throwing a party for 150 people is not cheap. I told Jody that we could just fly to Munich instead. We could, in truth, spend a week in Bavaria for less than it would cost to throw one party. Plus, we'd have better beer and an actual German atmosphere.

Jody's response stopped me cold: "This party is a different kind of moment."

She was right. The trip to Munich would have been enjoyable. But the biergarten party is a symbol. It's the visible reminder that our community matters to us, that friendship requires investment, that some things are worth the cost even when the economics don't compute.

We've built other symbols too. Since 2015, we've hosted a holiday brunch where friends, neighbors, and colleagues can all gather in one place. The invitation list keeps growing because making time for everyone individually has become impossible. The brunch says, "You matter to us, and this is the moment we've created to prove it."

On New Year's Eve, we don't stay up until midnight. Instead, we go to a British pub with friends around noon and celebrate New Year's at 4 PM when the clock strikes midnight in London. Bagpipes play. Toasts are made. Everyone gets home to their families by early evening, safe and warm, rather than driving through crowds at 1 AM.

These aren't corporate initiatives. They're symbols we've created for our own lives. The biergarten. The holiday brunch. The 4 PM New Year's toast. Each one is a visible reminder of what we value.

I've even transformed Christmas. But that transformation came from pain, not planning.

My Grandma Re would always host Christmas Eve when I was growing up. It was my favorite night of the year. She had divorced my Papa Jack when I was young, so the families did Christmas Eve with her and Christmas Day with him. Her house, her food, her warmth. That was the moment I looked forward to all December.

When she passed away suddenly a few years ago, we tried to recreate that magic the following Christmas Eve. The traditions were the same and so were the intentions. But it was awful. The absence was everywhere. We were going through motions that belonged to someone who was gone.

The next year, I decided we needed something completely new. Our own fresh moment. Christmas Eve became poker night with Chinese food and a toast to *A Christmas Story*, a family favorite movie. Christmas Day at my parents' house, which used to mean sitting around awkwardly after presents, now features games of chance I design for adults and kids alike.

The symbol shifted from inherited tradition to intentional creation. We couldn't sustain what Grandma Re had built. But we could build something new that honored the spirit of what she gave us: a reason to gather, a reason to laugh, a moment worth protecting.

What are your symbols? What visible reminders have you created for the values you claim to hold? If the answer is "none," that's a sustainability problem. Values without symbols fade. Intentions without rituals dissolve.

Succession: Culture That Outlives You

Before anyone can become a member of the Vienna Philharmonic, they must first successfully audition for the Vienna State Opera Orchestra, a sort of minor league version of the Philharmonic. Then they must perform with that orchestra for a minimum of three years, demonstrating their capability. Only after this probationary period can a musician even request an application for the Philharmonic.[96]

The process takes years. It's deliberately slow. Because the Vienna Philharmonic isn't just selecting talented musicians. They're selecting musicians who have absorbed the sound, the style, the culture that makes the Philharmonic distinctive.

This is succession by immersion. New members don't learn the Vienna sound from a manual. They learn it by playing for years alongside those who already embody it, before being entrusted with membership.

Costco operates similarly. Ron Vachris spent forty-two years at the company before becoming CEO.[97] Craig Jelinek spent twenty-eight years before him. Jim Sinegal founded the company and then led it for twenty-eight years himself. Leadership transitions at Costco aren't events. They're the culmination of decades of culture being transmitted from generation to generation.

When Vachris defended Costco's values against political pressure in 2025, he wasn't making a bold move. He was doing what forty-two years of absorption had prepared him to do.[98] The succession plan had worked because the culture had been transmitted.

Most organizations treat succession as a staffing problem. Who has the skills? Who has the experience? Who can execute the strategy?

The Vienna Philharmonic and Costco treat succession as a culture problem. Who has absorbed the values? Who will defend the symbols? Who will tell the stories to the next generation?

This distinction explains why most moment design initiatives fail at the eighteen-month mark I described in chapter 12. The leader who championed the initiative moved on. The successor has different priorities. The systems weren't embedded deeply enough. The stories weren't captured. The symbols weren't established. The next leader inherited a project, not a culture.

Sustainable moments require thinking about who comes next before the current chapter ends.

I saw this principle embodied in a nonprofit whose board I served on for several years: Working Wardrobes in Orange County. The organization helps people who are homeless, survivors of domestic violence, veterans, and others facing barriers to employment. They don't just provide job training. They provide transformation.

The culmination of their program is a Saturday graduation event that I participated in many times. Clients who had completed the program would come in that morning and have their hair done by volunteer stylists. Then personal shoppers, me included, would help them select professional clothes from donated wardrobes. Not just any clothes. Quality clothes. The kind you'd wear to an interview in which you wanted to be taken seriously.

Being a personal shopper was one of my favorite things to do. I'd work with someone who had been through hardship I could barely imagine, and I'd help them see themselves differently. I was overcome every time the moment came when they'd look in the mirror and see themselves dressed for success and ready for interviews we'd also helped them prepare for. It was a culmination moment designed with intention.

The ceremony at the end was powerful. Graduates would walk out in their new suits or dresses, their hair done, their heads high, to applause from staff and volunteers. Some cried. Many had never experienced that kind of public recognition for anything.

When graduates got jobs, the staff would celebrate with them at the office. And here's what really demonstrated the sustainability: many graduates came back to volunteer, helping others walk the same path they had walked. The moment created more moments. The system perpetuated itself.

Working Wardrobes has served over 125,000 people since 1990. Their founder, Jerri Rosen, retired in recent years, but the organization continues. Why? Because the moment wasn't about Jerri. It was about a system of transformation that could be passed from one generation of staff and volunteers to the next. The graduation ceremony, the personal shopping experience, the dignity of the process. All of it was designed to be repeatable, sustainable, independent of any single person.

That's what succession looks like in practice.

The Four Killers of Momentum

I've watched hundreds of organizations launch moment initiatives with energy and enthusiasm, and I've watched those initiatives fade. The patterns repeat so consistently I can name them.

Harvard professor John Kotter spent a decade studying over one hundred companies attempting major transformations. His findings, published in the *Harvard Business Review*, identified eight errors that doom change efforts.[99] The eighth and final error? Not anchoring changes in the corporation's culture. Organizations would launch initiatives, see initial success, declare victory, and move on. Within a few years, the changes would inevitably evaporate. The old ways would return because no one had built the systems, stories, symbols, and succession plans to make the changes permanent.

Kotter found that organizations need roughly 75 percent of management aligned and committed in order to sustain change past the initiation stage. That's a high bar. It means momentum isn't optional. It's mathematical. Without critical mass, gravity wins.

The specific killers I see most often fall into four categories:

- **Leader Fatigue.** The person who championed the initiative burns out or moves on. Without a succession plan, the momentum disappears with them. The champion's energy had been holding everything together. When they stop pushing, everything stops moving.

- **Competing Priorities.** Quarterly pressure crowds out moment work. When the CFO asks about this quarter's numbers and the "soft stuff" starts looking expendable, executives make seemingly rational short-term choices that destroy long-term culture. The Moments Audit from chapter 11 becomes a memory. The design principles from chapter 12 become nice ideas we'll get back to "when things calm down."

- **New Employee Dilution.** The people who weren't there for the original transformation don't feel the same ownership. They inherited something they didn't build. Without intentional onboarding into the moment culture, without the stories being told and the symbols being explained, new employees treat the initiatives as someone else's project.

- **Success Amnesia.** Things are working, but we stop doing what made them work. The discipline that created the results feels unnecessary once the results arrive. We forget that a healthy culture requires constant attention. We start taking the moments for granted, treating them as natural rather than intentional, inevitable rather than designed.

Luckily for us, each of these killers has an antidote.

Leader fatigue requires distributed ownership. Don't be the Vienna Philharmonic's conductor. Be the Vienna Philharmonic's system. Build moment design into multiple people's responsibilities, not just the champion's passion project.

Competing priorities require structural protection. Costco's hot dog price isn't subject to quarterly review. Some things have to be declared off-limits, protected from the normal optimization pressures that kill long-term thinking.

New employee dilution requires intentional onboarding. Don't just tell new people what to do. Tell them why. Share the stories. Explain the symbols. The Vienna Philharmonic doesn't hand musicians an instrument and say, "Play." New recruits spend years in an adjacent role, absorbing the culture before being trusted with full membership.

Success amnesia requires constant measurement. Not to prove value to skeptics but to remind yourself what's working. The Moments Audit from chapter 11 shouldn't be a one-time exercise. Run it annually. The gaps you discover will remind you that the work isn't done.

Beyond Organizations: Sustaining Personal Moments

Everything I've said about organizational sustainability applies to personal relationships, family traditions, friendships, and community bonds.

Friendships, for instance, fade when we stop creating systems for connection. "We should get together sometime" turns into years of silence. The intention was real. The system was missing.

That's why the *biergarten* matters. That's why the holiday brunch matters. They're not just parties. They're systems for maintaining relationships that would otherwise drift apart through the gravitational pull of busy lives.

Think about your closest friendships. The ones that have lasted decades. I'd bet they have systems, even if you don't call them that. The annual trip. The standing dinner date. The text thread that never goes quiet. Something structural that creates repeated moments of connection.

Now think about friendships that have faded. The people you were once close to who are now names you scroll past on social media. What's missing? Usually, it's simple: no system. No regular rhythm of contact. Just good intentions that slowly dissolve.

The same applies to family.

Traditions are systems disguised as rituals. The families with the strongest bonds aren't lucky. They've built infrastructure for togetherness. The annual vacation to the same place. The Sunday dinner that everyone attends. The holiday ritual that everyone knows, with stories told every year until the youngest child can recite them from memory.

When I transformed Christmas Eve into a poker night and Christmas Day into a games day, I was building systems. The awkward gathering became an intentional moment. And because the new tradition is enjoyable, it creates its own momentum. People look forward to it. The system sustains itself.

What about your neighbors? Your community? The people who live on your street but whom you only wave to from the driveway?

Neighbors become friends through repeated moments of connection. The holiday brunch we host includes neighbors alongside colleagues and friends. Some of those neighbors have become genuine friends, people who check on us when we travel, who text about packages left on our porch, who feel like community instead of strangers who happen to share a street.

That didn't happen by accident. It happened because we created a system for connection. The brunch became the infrastructure for relationships that wouldn't have formed otherwise.

Try this: Think about the next time you'll be with friends or family. Not a special occasion, just a regular gathering. What could you do to make it a true moment instead of just another get-together? The answer might be asking one question that goes deeper than small talk. Or one ritual, even a tiny one, that makes the gathering distinctive. Or one way to recognize someone who usually goes unnoticed. The systems don't have to be elaborate. They just have to be intentional.

The Warning Signs

How do you know when momentum is fading? The signs are predictable if you know what to watch for:

- **The stories stop spreading.** New employees don't know the origin stories. They've never heard about the moment that defined the culture. They know what to do but not why.

- **The symbols become checkboxes.** The ritual continues but the meaning has drained out. People go through the motions. Recognition moments become formulaic. The *biergarten* becomes a chore instead of a joy.

- **Exceptions multiply.** "We'll skip it this year because of the budget." "We'll simplify it because people are busy." Each exception seems reasonable in isolation. Collectively, they represent momentum dying.

- **New leaders question the basics.** "Why do we spend so much on this?" "What's the ROI?" "Couldn't we be more efficient?" These questions aren't illegitimate. But when they're asked about foundational moments, they signal that succession has failed. The new leader inherited the practice but not the purpose.

- **People ask, "Remember when?"** Nostalgia for past moments indicates that present moments aren't creating the same impact. "Remember when we used to...?" means the current version has lost something essential. The stories being told are all from the past. Nothing from this year makes the highlight reel.

- **The metrics improve but the feeling changes.** This is the sneakiest warning sign. Efficiency can destroy moments even while improving measurable outcomes. The recognition program takes less time to run but no longer feels meaningful. The onboarding process is smoother but no longer creates belonging. The numbers look good. The magic is gone.

When you see these signs, you have a choice. You can let the momentum continue to fade. Or you can treat the warning as an invitation to rebuild.

The Recovery Protocol

Jan Carlzon knew he needed a "second wave" at Scandinavian Airlines when he saw just how steeply momentum had faded. It was time to relaunch what he'd already launched. If you too are witnessing a dip in momentum, it may be time for your own recovery measures.

Recovery follows these predictable steps:

1. Acknowledge the slip.
2. Return to the founding stories.
3. Reinforce the symbols that have eroded.
4. Rebuild the systems.
5. Celebrate the restart as its own moment.

Recovery isn't failure. It's maintenance. The Vienna Philharmonic has had periods when their distinctive sound had faded and needed to be consciously restored. The *biergarten* almost died and had to be recommitted to.

What matters isn't avoiding drift. It's recognizing it and choosing to return.

Full Circle

I started this book with a dinner where former employees told me that they'd give all the money back to be working in the company we had. That conversation launched every idea I've shared between that page and this one.

What Tim and Sasha missed wasn't a single moment. It was a sustained culture of moments. Twenty years of inception experiences that made people feel valued from day one. Transition support that helped people navigate change. Recognition that came from peers, not just management. Truth delivered with care. Connections that changed how people related to each other. Culminations that honored endings before rushing to beginnings.

The seven moment types from part two weren't academic categories. They were the architecture of what made that company worth mourning.

The culture wasn't sustained by accident. We had systems, even if I didn't call them that. The handwritten holiday cards were a system that stretched to over 3,500 cards by its final year and started in October because there was no other way to get them done. The military spouse support program was a system that involved paying people during their relocations without touching their PTO. The transparency about financials was a system that included sharing numbers that most CEOs keep hidden. The peer recognition infrastructure was a system built on bottom-up appreciation that caught what top-down oversight missed.

We had stories. The Texas power outage story. The "almost lost our biggest client but we stayed until 2 AM" story. The stories got told at all-hands meetings and during onboarding and over drinks after work.

We had symbols. The cards themselves were symbols. The way we handled crises became symbols. The company meetings that always started with personal check-ins before business became symbols.

What we didn't have was succession. I didn't build for the exit. I built for me being there. When I left, the systems went with me. The stories stopped being told. The symbols lost their protector. The culture that Tim and Sasha mourned couldn't survive my departure because I hadn't built it to survive my departure.

That's the lesson I learned too late to apply at PeopleG2. But it's not too late for you.

Your Sustainability Audit

Before we move to the final chapter, take stock. Answer these questions honestly:

- **Systems.** What infrastructure have you built for moments? Are those moments dependent on you, or can they continue without you? Could someone else run the recognition program, design the onboarding experience, facilitate the truth conversations? If you disappeared tomorrow, what would survive?

- **Stories.** What founding stories define your culture? Can new members tell those stories accurately? Are they documented anywhere, or do they live only in the memories of people who were there?

- **Symbols.** What visible reminders reinforce your values? What rituals, artifacts, or traditions make your culture tangible? If someone were to visit for a day, what would they see that demonstrates what you believe?

- **Succession.** Who is being prepared to carry this forward? Who understands not just what you do but also why? Who would defend the culture if it came under pressure?

The way the Vienna Philharmonic answers these questions is how it's sustained excellence for 180-plus years. The way Costco answers is why their culture survived three CEO transitions and political pressure that would have broken other companies.

How do your answers compare?

This is your Build for the Exit audit. The Vienna Philharmonic passes it. Costco passes it. Does your organization? Does your family? Do you?

The audit from chapter 11 identified where you're failing to create moments. The design principles from chapter 12 showed you how to be intentional about moments. This chapter has shown you how to make moments last.

What remains is the choice itself. Not whether to design moments; you're already doing that whether you realize it or not. Not whether to build systems; you have them or you'll watch your culture fade. The choice is whether to be intentional about all of it, to see the architecture of moments clearly and build it deliberately.

Chapter 14 will make that choice explicit. But for now, sit with this: The dinner that broke me open at the beginning of this book wasn't about what we built at PeopleG2. It was about what didn't survive after I left. The people who would give all the money back were mourning something that could have been sustained if I'd thought differently about sustainability.

You have the chance to build what lasts. Not because you'll live forever but because you can create moments that do.

The Vienna Philharmonic is proof. It has shined for 184 years and counting.[100] Through wars, revolutions, economic collapses, and pandemics. The sound persists. The culture endures. The moments continue.

What will persist from your work? From your leadership? From your relationships? From your family traditions? From the moments you're creating right now?

Not everything. That's the honest answer. Not everything will last. But some things can. The question is whether you're building for permanence or hoping for luck.

Yes, your moments matter. But will they matter after you're gone?

"How we spend our days
is, of course, how we
spend our lives."
ANNIE DILLARD

THIS IS YOUR MOMENT: EMBRACE IT

Here's something I don't often admit. After building a company, after writing books about culture and leadership, after standing on stages telling other people how to create meaningful work, I still wonder whether I'm getting it right. I still miss moments. I still catch myself checking my phone when someone needs my full attention. I still optimize when I should be taking it hard.

Last week, my wife, Jody, asked me a question over dinner. I don't remember the exact question. Instead, I remember realizing, mid-answer, that I wasn't really there. My body was at the table, but my mind was somewhere else. Jody noticed. She didn't say anything, though. She didn't have to.

That's the gap between knowing and doing. I've written this book about moments that matter, and I still miss them. I teach managers how to show up with presence, and I still drift. I'm here telling you about the Third Space, and I still rush through without preparation.

I'm telling you this because the question that haunts me is probably the same one that haunts you: am I showing up as the best version of myself in the moments that matter most?

Not consistently. Not every day. Not in everything. In the moments that will be remembered. In the roles I've chosen to prioritize. In the relationships I've decided matter most.

That question is why I wrote this book. Not because I've mastered moments. Because I'm still learning to see them.

The Best of Times

I started this book with that cold night in Oregon when a conversation with two former employees broke me open because it revealed what I'd been chasing without knowing it. It wasn't just a great place to work or an exceptional culture. It wasn't competitive benefits or impressive retention rates.

The thing I'd been chasing was a singular vision: creating the best place my employees would ever work. In their whole careers.

That's my North Star now. And while I've spent most of this book talking about work, the principles that create the best workplace also extend far beyond the office. Moments are how you become the best at whatever you choose to prioritize.

I'm not asking you to be the best at everything. No one can be. You can't be the best CEO and the best parent and the best spouse and the best friend and the best neighbor and the best sibling and the best mentor all at once. That way lies exhaustion and failure.

But you can choose. You can decide which roles matter most to you. And in those roles, in the moments that define them, you can show up as the best version of yourself.

Maybe work isn't your arena. Maybe you're reading this book because you want to be the best parent your kids will ever have. Not a good parent. The one they'll look back on and say, "My mom showed up for me in ways I didn't even understand until I became a parent myself." Or, "My dad was there. Really there. When it mattered."

Maybe you want to be the best friend. The one who shows up with a toolbox instead of saying, "Let me know if you need anything." The one who brings chicken piccata every Friday during the crisis. The one people call when everything falls apart because they know you'll actually be there.

Maybe you want to be the best spouse. Not perfect. Not romantic-comedy ideal. The one who notices when something is wrong before it's spoken. The one who chooses the hard conversation over the easy silence. The one who, decades from now, will be remembered as having made the marriage feel like the best of times.

Maybe you want to be the best neighbor. The one who transforms a street of strangers into an actual community. The one who hosts the *biergarten*, who remembers names, who makes the neighborhood feel like somewhere people belong rather than just somewhere they live.

The arena doesn't matter. The principle is the same.

Think about the difference between good and best. Good parents provide for their children. Best parents create moments their children will carry for life. Good friends are there when asked. Best friends show up before being asked. Good spouses keep the peace. Best spouses tell the truth wrapped in care. Good neighbors wave from the driveway. Best neighbors build something that feels like home.

The gap between good and best isn't time or resources. It's moments. The willingness to see them. The presence to shape them. The discipline to scale them.

Choose your arena. Then make it the best of times for the people in it.

Three Questions

Before you close this book, I want you to sit with three questions. Don't answer them quickly. Sit with them.

The Oregon Question. What five moments will people remember about you? Not what you accomplished. Not your title or your possessions or your social media presence. What specific moments will they describe when they're trying to explain who you were? What will your employees say? Your children? Your spouse? Your friends? When they gather for dinner ten years from now, what stories will they tell? If you can't name five, or if the ones you name aren't the ones you'd want, you know where to start.

The Uncle Lee Question. Which moment is hiding inside the obvious one? In chapter 2, I told you about the talent show. The TV performance, the third-place finish, the Hollywood experience. None of that was the moment. The moment was a dying man in a green room who showed up for his nephew when he could have stayed home. What obvious moments are you celebrating while missing the real ones underneath? The graduation ceremony or the conversation from last night? The wedding day or the drive home from the hospital after the diagnosis? The promotion announcement or the quiet Tuesday when someone believed in you before you believed in yourself?

The Take-It-Hard Question. Where are you optimizing when you should be choosing difficulty? Consider the text instead of the phone call. Or the gift card instead of the thoughtful gift. Maybe it's the "we should get together sometime" instead of the date on the calendar. Or the efficient path instead of the meaningful one. Where in your life are you taking it easy when the moment demands everything you have?

I ask myself these questions regularly. The answers still surprise me. I still find gaps between who I want to be and how I'm actually showing up.

That's not failure. That's practice.

What I Got Wrong

I spent twenty years building PeopleG2. There, we created a culture that employees would trade their now-higher salaries to return to. We had the moments. We had the stories. We had everything I've written about in this book.

And when I sold the company and walked away, too much of it left with me.

The handwritten holiday cards? Those were my thing. The generators during the Texas power outage? That decision came from me. The way we handled failures, the transparency about finances, the peer recognition that caught what top-down oversight missed? All of it was filtered through my presence.

The first time I heard that the new owners had canceled the holiday cards, I felt it in my chest before I understood it in my head. Something precious was disappearing. Something I'd built but failed to protect.

I didn't build for sustainability. I built a culture that depended on me being there to sustain it. When that chapter ended, the moments my former employees mourned couldn't survive my departure.

Chapter 13 was about building for the exit: Systems, Stories, Symbols, and Succession. The Vienna Philharmonic has sustained their sound for 184 years because they embedded their culture into infrastructure that outlasts any individual. Costco maintained their values through three CEO transitions because they built something that doesn't depend on the founder being in the room.

I didn't do that. I learned that lesson too late to apply it at PeopleG2.

But it's not too late for you.

Whatever moments you're creating, in whatever arena you've chosen, ask yourself, "Will this survive my absence?" If you're building a family culture, will your children carry it to their own families? If you're the glue in a friendship group, have you taught others to hold it together? If you're the one who always organizes the neighborhood gatherings, have you made it easy for someone else to continue?

The question isn't whether your moments matter. Every chapter of this book has proven that they do. The question is whether they'll matter after you're gone.

The Stories That Stay

I still think about Uncle Lee in that green room. Forty years later, the TV performance is a blur. The lights, the costume, the lip-syncing to "We Built This City," the third-place finish. I can recall the facts, but I can't feel them anymore. They're data, not memory.

What I can feel is him sitting there. Under the fluorescent lights. Inside, the smell of hairspray and anticipation. We talked about nothing important. School. My broken arm from falling off his horse Rick the year before. His other horse, Jerry, and how gentle Jerry was compared to Rick. Normal uncle stuff.

I didn't know it would be the last time I'd see him. But he knew. He had lung cancer. Everyone had told me he couldn't make it to the taping. But there he was. He was dying, and he came anyway.

That's the moment inside the moment. I missed it for decades because I was focused on the obvious thing instead of the real thing.

I still think about Jody in those hospital rooms.

The strokes. Six surgeries. The doctors who ran out of rooms when I had questions and the doctors who sat down and said, "I don't know, but let's figure it out." The hundreds of hours of research so I could be prepared when the moment demanded it. Standing up when it would have been so much easier to sit down.

Taking it hard meant being willing to be difficult. It meant fighting with medical professionals when consensus pointed the wrong direction. It meant doing the preparation in the Third Space so that when the crucial conversation came, I could show up as the most prepared non-medical person in the room.

She's here today because someone refused to take it easy when her life was on the line.

I still think about flying over the Pacific with three engines failing.

We were on our way to Russia to bring home our daughter, Luba. The plane lost three of its four engines. For a period of time I don't like to calculate, we were falling toward an ocean that would have swallowed us without a trace.

I think about that flight when I'm tempted to take the easy path. Adoption was the hard choice. Flying across the world to bring home a child from an orphanage was the hard choice. Almost dying in the process was not part of the plan, but it reminded me what we were willing to risk for something that mattered.

Luba is grown now. The choice to take it hard created a family.

I still think about Papa Jack falling asleep in the passenger seat.

I was fifteen with a learner's permit. He came over to let me practice driving. We got in the car, I started down the street, and he tilted his seat back to take a nap.

"What are you doing?" I asked.

"I know you got this," he assured, "I might as well take a nap."

Can you imagine giving someone that much confidence? Demonstrating your belief in them by falling asleep, not worrying one bit that they might crash the car or make a mistake? He was there if I needed him. But he trusted me so completely that he saw no reason to stay awake and supervise.

I drove for hours that day. And the whole time, Papa Jack snored away in the passenger seat, giving me probably the greatest gift of confidence I've ever received.

Thirty-five years later, every time I trust someone before they've fully earned it, I think of him snoring in that passenger seat. Every time I choose belief over supervision, that's thanks to Papa Jack.

These are the stories that stay. Not because I engineered them. Not because I followed a framework. Because someone showed up fully when showing up mattered.

Uncle Lee showed up dying. Jody's doctors showed up uncertain but willing. I showed up on that plane terrified but committed. Papa Jack showed up ready to trust me.

The showing up is the thing.

The Practice

I don't have a thirty-day challenge for you. You've had thirteen chapters of frameworks and tools and practical applications. You have enough systems.

What I have is a practice made up of five commitments I make to myself. Maybe they'll mean something to you too. Every day, try committing to one or more until all five become instinct:

I will see the moment hiding inside the obvious one.

I will show up fully when showing up matters.

I will take it hard when taking it easy would cost what I can't afford to lose.

I will build something that outlasts my presence.

I will see the moment when I'm inside the moment.

This is practice, not perfection. I will fail. I will miss moments. I will catch myself optimizing when I should be present, rushing when I should be still, checking my phone when someone needs my eyes.

The practice isn't about getting it right every time. It's about returning to the principles that reflect my values and the person I want to be. Again and again. Until the person I want to be is very nearly indistinguishable from the person I am.

One More Story

A friend of mine went through a divorce recently.

We're not best friends. We're the kind of friends who see each other a few times a year, who text occasionally, who care about each other without being in each other's daily lives.

I heard about the divorce through mutual friends. The normal response would have been to send a text. "Let me know if you need anything." The seven useless words from chapter 8.

Instead, I called. Not because I had anything profound to say. Not because I could fix anything. Just to listen.

We talked for an hour. He cried. I mostly listened. At the end, he said something that stuck with me.

"I didn't expect you to call. Most people just text."

Most people just text.

Figure 14.1. Most people just text. You can call.

That's the gap. That's where moments hide. In the space between what most people do and what the situation actually requires.

The text was efficient. The call was a moment.

The text said, "I'm thinking about you." The call said, "You matter enough for me to stop what I'm doing and be with you."

I didn't follow a framework. I didn't consult a tool kit. I just asked myself the question, "What would taking it easy look like?" The answer, of course, was a text. What would taking it hard look like? A call.

And then I chose.

That's all this is. Seeing the moment. Choosing the harder path. Showing up.

Most people just text. You can call.

For ongoing resources, discussion guides, and updates, visit chrisdyer.com/moments.

APPENDIX: MOMENTS QUICK REFERENCE

The Seven Moment Types at a Glance

Inception Moments (chapter 4): First days, first meetings, first impressions. You have 100 milliseconds before judgments lock in. Design the beginning deliberately.

Transition Moments (chapter 5): The space between what was and what's next. Use the Third Space to arrive as your best self. The transition is where transformation happens.

Decision Moments (chapter 6): When the path forks and someone is watching. Your choices under pressure become the stories people tell about you.

Recognition Moments (chapter 7): Acknowledgment that changes how someone sees themselves. Requires specificity, timeliness, and the right ratio. Peer-to-peer often works better than top-down.

Connection Moments (chapter 8): When two people share something true, feel heard, and leave with next steps. Most people just text. You can call.

Truth Moments (chapter 9): Delivering difficult information with care. The truth delivered today won't be received today. Create safety first, deliver truth second, provide support third.

Culmination Moments (chapter 10): Endings that become origins. Honor what's ending before reaching for what's beginning. Let your hands tremble.

Before Key Moments: Quick Prompts

Before a new hire's first day, ask yourself, "What will they see, hear, and feel in the first hour? Who will greet them? What story will they tell tonight?"

Before a difficult conversation, ask yourself, "Have I created safety? Am I delivering truth or judgment? What support will I offer afterward?"

Before a major transition, ask yourself, "Have I used the Third Space? Am I arriving from what just happened, or am I present for what's next?"

Before recognizing someone, ask yourself, "Is this specific enough that only they could receive it? Am I acknowledging who they are, not just what they did?"

Before an ending, ask yourself, "Am I rushing past this to get to the next thing? What deserves to be honored here?"

When Something Falls Flat: Diagnostic

The moment didn't land.

- Did I identify it as a moment at all, or did it pass unnoticed?

- Was I fully present, or was I already thinking about what would come next?

- Did I let it fade, or did I help it become a story?

The recognition felt hollow.

- Was it specific, or could anyone have received it?

- Was it timely, or had the moment passed?

- Did it come from the right person?

The truth conversation backfired.

- Did I establish safety first?

- Did I deliver truth or judgment?

- Did I give them time to process before expecting a response?

The connection attempt felt forced.

- Did both people share something true?

- Did both people feel heard?

- Were there clear next steps?

The transition left me rattled.

- Did I use the Third Space, or did I carry the last moment into this one?

- Did I prepare for what this moment needed?

The Core Frameworks

See, Shape, Scale: Identify moments before they happen. Show up fully when they arrive. Help them become stories that spread.

Third Space: The transition between where you were and where you're going. Use it to shed the residue of the last moment and arrive prepared for the next.

Take It Hard: When a moment matters, choose the harder path. Picture stairs over elevators. Handwritten notes over typed ones. Calls over texts. The inefficient choice often carries the most weight.

The 5:1 Ratio: It takes five positive interactions to counteract every negative one. In relationships, in teams, in cultures. The math applies everywhere.

Build for the Exit: Prioritize Systems, Stories, Symbols, and Succession. Moments that depend on you being there won't survive your absence.

Warning Signs You're Missing Moments

- You're optimizing for efficiency in situations that call for significance.

- You're treating beginnings as formalities instead of foundations.

- You're rushing past endings to reach new beginnings.

- You're delivering recognition that could apply to anyone.

- You're choosing a text when a call is what the moment requires.

- You're carrying the residue of the last meeting into the next one.

- You're letting stories fade instead of helping them spread.

For More Resources

Visit chrisdyer.com/moments for:

- Downloadable Moments Audit worksheet

- Discussion guides for teams

- Video examples of each moment type

- Updates and new research

ACKNOWLEDGMENTS

This book exists because of a cold night in Oregon and two people brave enough to tell me what they really felt. Tim and Sasha, you probably don't know that our conversation launched the journey that became these pages. Thank you for your honesty. It changed everything.

Pete Sheahan: You've been my mentor, my thinking partner, and the person who heard me describe that dinner and said, "That's the most interesting thing you've ever said to me." Twenty-five minutes later, we had the framework. Now we have a book. Your fingerprints are on every chapter.

Connor Trombley: You were in that room with Pete and me when the ideas started flying. Your ability to distill the wisdom of giants into something actionable shaped this framework from the beginning. This book is sharper because of you.

James: You looked me in the eye and told me that maybe I wasn't the right person to be CEO. That truth moment shaped not just chapter 9 but also how I think about courage in relationships. Thank you for caring enough to say what others wouldn't.

Uncle Lee and Papa Jack: You're both gone now, but you're alive in these pages. Uncle Lee, you showed me what it means to show up when showing up costs everything. Papa Jack, you showed me what radical belief looks like, even if it meant falling asleep in the passenger seat while a fifteen-year-old drove. I carry you both with me.

My wife, Jody: You read every word first. You were my first cheerleader and my first critic, often in the same sentence. You survived six surgeries and taught me what taking it hard really means. You've lived these principles with me, challenged me when I forgot them, and loved me through the moments I got wrong. This book is as much yours as it is mine.

My children: Thank you for giving me stories worth telling and for forgiving me when I missed moments I should have caught. You've taught me more about inception, transition, and connection than any research ever could.

My friends and family: I wrote this book in a month. One month of ignoring phone calls, skipping dinners, and disappearing into my office while the rest of life waited. Thank you for waiting. Thank you for understanding. Thank you for being there when I finally emerged.

My employees, past and present: You lived these ideas with me before they had names. You trusted me with your careers, your growth, and your moments. The culture we built together is the proof that these principles work. I hope you see yourselves in these pages.

My parents, my coaches, and my teachers: You shaped me before I knew I was being shaped. The values in this book started with you. Every lesson about showing up, working hard, and treating people right traces back to something you taught me, whether you remember teaching it or not.

Amelia Forczak and the entire Pithy Wordsmithery team: You helped me get this published faster than you've ever published any book before. Your skill, dedication, and belief in this project pushed it across the finish line. I'm grateful for every edit, every question, and every deadline you held me to.

My FCC crew and my SoCal Speakers Pod: You know who you are and what you mean to me.

My dear friends from ImpactEleven: You've shaped how I think about leadership, speaking, and showing up on stages around the world. The conversations we've had over the years echo throughout this book.

Josh Linkner, Seth Mattison, and Ryan Estis: Your thought leadership has challenged and inspired me. Watching how you think, create, and contribute to the world has made me a better speaker and a better writer.

Finally, to everyone who shared their stories with me, who let me learn from their moments, who trusted me with their vulnerabilities: This book is built on your generosity. The names may be changed, but the lessons are real.

Not all moments are created equal. Neither are the people who shape them. I've been fortunate to have the right people in the moments that mattered most.

ABOUT THE AUTHOR

Chris Dyer is a serial entrepreneur who spent twenty years learning how to build companies that people actually want to work for. His firm, PeopleG2, earned "Best Place to Work" recognition fifteen times and landed on the Inc. 5000 list of fastest-growing companies five times. Not because he had it figured out from the start but because he kept failing and fixing and failing again until the culture finally stuck.

Then came a dinner that changed everything. Former employees told him that they'd "give all the money back" to return to his company. Not for the salaries. For the moments that made them feel like they mattered. That conversation became the seed for this book.

Inc. Magazine named Chris the #1 Leadership Speaker on Culture, and he has delivered more than 300 keynotes across twenty-plus countries, helping organizations understand that culture isn't built through ping-pong tables or mission statements. It's built in moments. The ones we notice. The ones we miss. And the ones we have the chance to create if we're paying attention.

He is the bestselling author of *The Power of Company Culture* and *Remote Work*, and has been working at the intersection of AI and workplace performance since 2018. His ideas have appeared in more than 500 media features worldwide.

Chris lives in Southern California with his wife. He's a father of three children adopted from Russia, now grown, and is a grandfather who finds that the lessons in this book matter even more at home than they do on stage.

ENDNOTES

1. Tor Nørretranders, *The User Illusion: Cutting Consciousness Down to Size* (New York: Penguin Books, 1998), 124–26.
2. Daniel L. Schacter, *The Seven Sins of Memory: How the Mind Forgets and Remembers* (Boston: Houghton Mifflin, 2001), 14–27.
3. James L. McGaugh, "Memory Consolidation and the Amygdala: A Systems Perspective," *Trends in Neurosciences* 25, no. 9 (2002): 456–61.
4. Brené Brown, *Daring Greatly: How the Courage to Be Vulnerable Transforms the Way We Live, Love, Parent, and Lead* (New York: Gotham Books, 2012), 198–99.
5. Chip Heath and Dan Heath, *The Power of Moments: Why Certain Experiences Have Extraordinary Impact* (New York: Simon & Schuster, 2017), 12–15.
6. John Gottman and Nan Silver, *The Seven Principles for Making Marriage Work* (New York: Crown, 1999), 67–68.
7. "Boeing 737 MAX Crashes," Aviation Safety Network, accessed November 2024, https://aviation-safety.net/database.
8. House Committee on Transportation and Infrastructure, Final Committee Report: The Design, Development & Certification of the Boeing 737 MAX (Washington, DC: US Government Publishing Office, 2020), 238.
9. *The Last Dance*, episode 7, directed by Jason Hehir, aired May 10, 2020, on ESPN.
10. Phil Jackson, *Eleven Rings: The Soul of Success* (New York: Penguin Press, 2013), 178.
11. Steve Kerr, interview by Dan Patrick, "The Dan Patrick Show," June 21, 2012.
12. Alan Deutschman, *Change or Die: The Three Keys to Change at Work and in Life* (New York: Harper Business, 2007), 1–3.
13. Erin Reid and Lakshmi Ramarajan, "Managing the High-Intensity Workplace," *Harvard Business Review* 94, no. 6 (2016), 84–90.
14. Dermot Crowley, *Urgent!: How to Focus on What Matters* (Milton, Queensland: John Wiley & Sons, 2020), 45–47.

15. Gustavo Razzetti, "The Problem with an Always Urgent Workplace Culture," Fearless Culture, accessed November 2024, https://www.fearlessculture.design.

16. James L. McGaugh, "Memory Consolidation and the Amygdala: A Systems Perspective," *Trends in Neurosciences* 25, no. 9 (2002), 456–61.

17. Elizabeth A. Kensinger, "Remembering the Details: Effects of Emotion," *Emotion Review* 1, no. 2 (2009), 99–113.

18. Abraham Maslow, *Toward a Psychology of Being*, 3rd ed. (New York: John Wiley & Sons, 1999), 45.

19. Gina Keating, *Netflixed: The Epic Battle for America's Eyeballs* (New York: Portfolio, 2012), 23–41.

20. While specific competitor data is proprietary, industry analysis from IBISWorld's Background Check Services Report (2009–2011) showed significant market consolidation during this period, with aggressive marketers gaining share from conservative competitors.

21. Dr. Sophie Raine, What is Third Space? (Perlego, May 8, 2024) https://www.perlego.com/knowledge/study-guides/what-is-third-space.

22. McKinsey & Company, "The Value of Customer Experience, Quantified," McKinsey Insights, August 2016, https://www.mckinsey.com/capabilities/growth-marketing-and-sales/our-insights/the-value-of-customer-experience-quantified.

23. Denise Lee Yohn, "Why Customer Experience Is Key to Customer Retention During Economic Uncertainty," *Harvard Business Review*, March 15, 2023.

24. Stephen King, *On Writing: A Memoir of the Craft* (New York: Scribner, 2000), 73–76.

25. Tabitha King, interview with Susan Toepfer, "The Once and Future Tabitha King," *People*, December 1980.

26. Patricia Sellers, "The Business of Being Oprah," *Fortune*, April 1, 2002.

27. Oprah Winfrey, commencement address at Harvard University, Cambridge, MA, May 30, 2013.

28. Janine Willis and Alexander Todorov, "First Impressions: Making Up Your Mind After a 100-ms Exposure to a Face," *Psychological Science* 17, no. 7 (2006): 592–98.

29. Alison Wood Brooks, "Get Excited: Reappraising Pre-Performance Anxiety as Excitement," *Journal of Experimental Psychology* 143, no. 3 (2014): 1144–58.

30. Nelson Mandela, *Long Walk to Freedom: The Autobiography of Nelson Mandela* (New York: Back Bay Books, 1995), 487–89.

31. John Carlin, *Playing the Enemy: Nelson Mandela and the Game That Made a Nation* (New York: Penguin Books, 2008), 95–97.

32. Danaan Parry, "The Parable of the Trapeze," in *Warriors of the Heart* (Bainbridge Island, WA: Earthstewards Network Publications, 1991), 84–85.

33. Ed Catmull and Amy Wallace, *Creativity, Inc.: Overcoming the Unseen Forces That Stand in the Way of True Inspiration* (New York: Random House, 2014), 213–17.

34. Theodore H. White, *The Making of the President 1960* (New York: Atheneum Publishers, 1961), 321–23.

35. David Garrow, *Bearing the Cross: Martin Luther King Jr. and the Southern Christian Leadership Conference* (New York: William Morrow, 1986), 142–49.

36. Lawrence Foster, *Robert Wood Johnson: The Gentleman Rebel* (State College, PA: Lillian Press, 1999), 456–78.

37. James Burke, interview by Mike Wallace, *60 Minutes*, CBS, December 5, 1982.

38. Tamara Kaplan, "The Tylenol Crisis: How Effective Public Relations Saved Johnson & Johnson," Pennsylvania State University, accessed November 2024, http://www.aerobiologicalengineering.com/wxk116/TylenolMurders/crisis.html.

39. Richard Tedlow, "The Tylenol Comeback," *Harvard Business Review*, Winter 1983.

40. Sarah Bradford, *Harriet Tubman: The Moses of Her People* (New York: Dover Publications, 2004), 89–92.

41. Ratherine Clinton, *Harriet Tubman: The Road to Freedom* (New York: Little, Brown and Company, 2004), 91.

42. Suzy Welch, *10-10-10: A Life-Transforming Idea* (New York: Scribner, 2009), 23–45.

43. Sheena Iyengar and Mark Lepper, "When Choice Is Demotivating: Can One Desire Too Much of a Good Thing?" Journal of Personality and Social Psychology 79, no. 6 (2000): 995–1006.

44. Tim Jackson, *Inside Intel: Andy Grove and the Rise of the World's Most Powerful Chip Company* (New York: Dutton, 1997), 201–3.

45. Andrew S. Grove, Only the Paranoid Survive: How to Exploit the Crisis Points That Challenge Every Company (New York: Currency Doubleday, 1996), 89.

46. John M. Gottman, *The Seven Principles for Making Marriage Work* (New York: Harmony Books, 1999), 26–34.

47. Marcial Losada and Emily Heaphy, "The Role of Positivity and Connectivity in the Performance of Business Teams," *American Behavioral Scientist* 47, no. 6 (2004): 740–65.

48. "The Lower Boundary of Workplace Mistreatment: Do Small Slights Matter?" *Proceedings of the National Academy of Sciences* 121 (2024).

49. James Kerr, *Legacy: What the All Blacks Can Teach Us About the Business of Life* (London: Constable, 2013), 19–22.

50. Ali Williams, "How the All Blacks Tradition of Sweeping the Sheds Began," RugbyPass, September 2020.

51. Dan Carter, *The Art of Winning* (London: Century, 2025), 67–71.

52. Jack Wiley and Brenda Kowske, *RESPECT: Delivering Results by Giving Employees What They Really Want* (San Francisco: Jossey-Bass, 2012), 84–89.

53. Doris Kearns Goodwin, *Team of Rivals: The Political Genius of Abraham Lincoln* (New York: Simon & Schuster, 2005), 318–22.

54. Nicholas Epley and Juliana Schroeder, "Mistakenly Seeking Solitude," *Journal of Experimental Psychology: General* 143, no. 5 (2014): 1980–99.

55. Priya Parker, *The Art of Gathering: How We Meet and Why It Matters* (New York: Riverhead Books, 2018).

56. Sidney Rosen and Abraham Tesser, "On Reluctance to Communicate Undesirable Information: The MUM Effect," *Sociometry* 33, no. 3 (1970): 253–63.

57. Amy C. Edmondson, *The Fearless Organization: Creating Psychological Safety in the Workplace for Learning, Innovation, and Growth* (Hoboken, NJ: Wiley, 2019), 15–18.

58. Kim Scott, *Radical Candor: Be a Kick-Ass Boss Without Losing Your Humanity* (New York: St. Martin's Press, 2017), 26–31.

59. Sheila Heen and Douglas Stone, *Thanks for the Feedback: The Science and Art of Receiving Feedback Well* (New York: Viking, 2014), 16–22.

60. The Triangle Shirtwaist Factory fire occurred on March 25, 1911, in New York City, killing 146 workers. Frances Perkins witnessed the tragedy from Washington Square. See Kirstin Downey, *The Woman Behind the New Deal: The Life of Frances Perkins, FDR's Secretary of Labor and His Moral Conscience* (New York: Anchor Books, 2009), 42–47.

61. A. F. G. Bell, *In Portugal* (London: John Lane, 1912). Bell describes *saudade* as "a vague and constant desire for something that does not and probably cannot exist, for something other than the present." Fado was added to the UNESCO Intangible Cultural Heritage Lists on November 27, 2011.

62. These untranslatable emotional concepts from various languages each describe specific emotional states that lack direct English equivalents: *Onsra* (Boro language, India), *Tu'burni* (Arabic), and *Mamihlapinatapai* (Yaghan, Chile).

63. "10 Things You Really Ought to Know about George Washington," Mount Vernon, accessed December 2024, https://www.mountvernon.org/george-washington/10-things-you-really-ought-to-know-about-george-washington.

64. Lee Habeeb, "Two Days Before Christmas, George Washington's Resignation Shocked the World," *Newsweek*, December 24, 2019.

65. David Howell's account of Washington's resignation appears in multiple historical records of the December 23, 1783, proceedings at the Maryland State House.

66. Daniel Kahneman et al., "When More Pain Is Preferred to Less: Adding a Better End," *Psychological Science* 4, no. 6 (1993): 401–5.

67. Steve Jobs, Stanford University commencement address, June 12, 2005, Stanford University.

68. "Derek Jeter's Final Yankee Stadium Game," MLB.com, February 10, 2023.

69. Roy F. Baumeister et al., "Bad Is Stronger Than Good," *Review of General Psychology* 5, no. 4 (2001): 323–70.

70. Columbia Accident Investigation Board, *Report, Volume 1* (Washington DC: Government Printing Office, 2003), 184.

71. McKinsey & Company, "This Time It's Personal: Shaping the 'New Possible' Through Employee Experience," September 30, 2021.

72. Gartner, "Creating a Connected Employee Experience," 2023.

73. Jan Carlzon, *Moments of Truth* (Cambridge, MA: Ballinger Publishing, 1987).

74. American Management Association 75th Anniversary Recognition of Management Developments.

75. Multiple sources on Walmart Germany failure: Mark Landler and Michael Barbaro, "No, Not Always," *New York Times*, August 2, 2006; Gerrit Wiesmann, "Why Wal-Mart Decided to Pack Its Bags in Germany," *Financial Times*, 2006.

76. Chip Heath and Dan Heath, *The Power of Moments* (New York: Simon & Schuster, 2017).

77. Daniel Kahneman, *Thinking, Fast and Slow* (New York: Farrar, Straus and Giroux, 2011).

78. Kim Scott, *Radical Candor* (New York: St. Martin's Press, 2017).

79. Betsy Allen-Manning, "National Workplace Trends Study," 2025.

80. Bill Taylor, "How One Fast-Food Chain Keeps Its Turnover Rates Absurdly Low," Harvard Business Review, 2016.

81. National Institute of Standards and Technology, "Pal's Sudden Service: Malcolm Baldrige National Quality Award Case Study," 2001.

82. McKinsey & Company, "Sustaining the Momentum of a Transformation," November 2016.

83. "Tradition," Vienna Philharmonic, accessed December 2024, https://www.wienerphilharmoniker.at/en/orchestra/tradition.

84. "History of the VPO," The Vienna Philharmonic Society, accessed December 2024, https://www.viennaphilharmonicsociety.org/about-us/history.

85. "The Vienna Philharmonic: One of the World's Great Orchestras," *Euronews*, July 14, 2022.

86. "Vienna Philharmonic Orchestra," Encyclopedia.com, accessed December 2024, https://www.encyclopedia.com/people/literature-and-arts/music-popular-and-jazz-biographies/vienna-philharmonic-orchestra.

87. Jake Rossen, "The Enduring Enigma of Costco's $1.50 Hot Dog and Soda Combo," Mental Floss, August 31, 2023.

88. Sam Kubota, "Report: Costco Co-Founder Told CEO He'd Kill Him If Price of Hot Dog Combo Went Up," Today.com, September 23, 2020.

89. "From Forklift Driver to CEO: Meet Costco's Ron Vachris," *Business Insider*, February 19, 2025.

90. "Costco Stands Resolute Against the Anti-DEI Movement," *Sustainability Magazine*, January 7, 2025.

91. Yasmin Gagne, "World Changing Ideas 2025: Why Costco CEO Ron Vachris is Fast Company's Visionary of the Year," *Fast Company*, June 17, 2025.

92. *Ibid.*

93. "Tradition," Vienna Philharmonic, accessed December 2024, https://www.wienerphilharmoniker.at/en/orchestra/tradition.

94. Paul J. Zak, "Why Inspiring Stories Make Us React: The Neuroscience of Narrative," *Cerebrum* (Dana Foundation, 2015); Paul J. Zak, "How Stories Change the Brain," *Greater Good Magazine*, December 17, 2013.

95. "The Vienna Philharmonic: One of the World's Great Orchestras," Euronews, July 14, 2022.

96. "History of the VPO," The Vienna Philharmonic Society, accessed December 2024, https://www.viennaphilharmonicsociety.org/about-us/history.

97. "From Forklift Driver to CEO: Meet Costco's Ron Vachris," *Business Insider*, February 19, 2025.

98. Donald Thompson, "Costco's DEI Defense is a Blueprint for Business Success and Leadership Excellence," WRAL.com, January 23, 2025.

99. John P. Kotter, "Leading Change: Why Transformation Efforts Fail," *Harvard Business Review*, May–June 1995.

100. McKinsey & Company, "Sustaining the Momentum of a Transformation," November 2016.

www.ingramcontent.com/pod-product-compliance
Lightning Source LLC
Chambersburg PA
CBHW032013150726
47990CB00005B/1947